The Streetcorner Strategy
for Winning Local Markets

The Streetcorner Strategy

for Winning Local Markets

Right Sales

Right Service

Right Customers

Right Cost

ROBERT E. HALL

Bard Press
AUSTIN, TEXAS

The Streetcorner Strategy for Winning Local Markets
Right Sales, Right Service, Right Customers, Right Cost

Bard Press
1515 Capital of Texas Highway S., Suite 107
Austin, Texas 78746
(512) 329-8373 fax (512) 329-6051
www.bardpress.com

ISBN 1-885167-37-7 paperback
ISBN 0-9639485-0-4 hardcover

The author may be contacted at the following address:

Robert E. Hall, CEO
ActionSystems Inc.
13155 Noel Road, Suite 1700
Dallas, Texas 75240
(972) 385-0680 fax (972) 239-3534

BARD PRESS
AUSTIN, TEXAS

Copyediting: Jeff Morris
Proofreading: Doris Dickey, Leslie Tingle
Text Design: Suzanne Pustejovsky
Jacket Design: RhodesStaffordWines Creative, Inc.
Composition/Production: Jeff Morris
Index: Linda Webster

Hardcover edition:
First printing, January 1994
Second printing, May 1994
Third printing, September 1994
Fourth printing, May 1995
Fifth printing, March 1996
Sixth printing, May 1997
Seventh printing, May 1999

Paperback edition:
First printing, May 1999

To Linda, Sarah, and Lauren.

CONTENTS

PART III

The Breakout Performer: Three Key Principles / **139**

FIGURES

TABLES

ACKNOWLEDGEMENTS

*A*LTHOUGH THIS BOOK BEARS MY NAME AS AUTHOR, I assure you it was a team effort. Let me tell you a little about the individual members of this excellent team.

Our firm, ActionSystems, began work on a process called Managing Local Markets in 1988. Since then we have studied, designed, developed, implemented, evaluated, and refined the process nonstop. This book outlines what we have learned about making local market management work. We had help.

As you might guess, it all started with a client. The Royal Bank of Canada — a $140 billion–asset bank with over 1,600 branches — asked us to work with them in developing a more effective approach to sales and service in the local market. Gwyn Gill, then Vice President of Marketing and Sales Planning at Royal, had real insight into the change required to make a large sales-and-service distribution system more proactive for the '90s. Jim Gannon guided us to design a business process that included training. Over time, Greg Bright, Dennice Leahey, Carolyn Burke, Fred Stark, Bruce Barch, Jackie Singh, and Judith Hatley all played key roles, and Gord Feeney, Senior Executive Vice President of the Retail Bank, has led the charge in making it a way of life across one of the largest branch systems in North America.

Along the way there have been a number of other clients who have successfully implemented local market management, and we have learned from each one. I would be remiss, however, not to thank Joel Epstein, Liz Flynn, and John Hartwell at Chase Manhattan Bank in New York for challenging us to tighten and refine the process and to apply it to the unique demographics of trade areas in Manhattan — commuters and all.

Within ActionSystems, Dawn Foster has been the force behind Managing Local Markets. She has been the chief doer and team manager of creation, installation, and refinement. No one in the company, including myself, can match her depth and breadth of experience; so much of what is in this book comes from her efforts. If there is a heaven for local market management, Dawn should be in charge there.

She has worked with an excellent team. Carol Farmer devised and implemented the initial model and continues to break new ground with her research and applications on lower-cost delivery practices for mass-market customers. Ronda Christopher brought years of experience from Neiman Marcus — a retailer that wrote the original book on serving high-value customers. Her practical experience and creative thinking added real innovation to the process. Marlene Sternjholm brought in-depth marketing information expertise, an unbelievable amount of energy, and a very practical view of how local market management should work. Joe Weilenbeck's work on sales management routines and Gregory LaMothe's research on market management practices have been instrumental in helping us develop the tools to sustain market management.

At ActionSystems we view Winning Local Markets as a movement. John Carter, Barbara Garber, Clay McKay, and Bob Rickert have done the tough missionary work of educating the marketplace. Reengineering and reallocating sales-and-service delivery to local market potential was not on the tip of the tongue of every client or prospect in 1988. Thanks, gang, for your passion, commitment, and success.

It is through all these efforts that I have been afforded the opportunity to write this book. Thanks to Dyan Moore, Mike Cooley, Leslie Guy, and Lisa Hunter for your untiring production support. Ray Bard, my publisher, and Jeff Morris, editor, were very helpful as they guided me through the mechanics of planning and writing a book. The biggest thanks of all in getting the book done goes to Marlene for managing me from beginning to end — always having the right next step, providing straight feedback and support, jumping in to help with titles and subtitles, and getting it done no matter how many other priorities she was juggling. If we ever go to war, I want Marlene on my side.

I owe a special thanks to Tom Morse, my partner; we started this journey together in 1979. The new software technology that Tom and his team are bringing to market and key account management is rapidly opening new horizons for what is possible at the local market level.

Finally, thanks to my soul mate and wife, Linda, for all the responsibilities that you took on so I could write this book.

INTRODUCTION

"The author who benefits you most is not
the one who tells you something you did not
already know, but the one who gives
expression to the truth that has been
dumbly struggling in you for utterance."[1]

— *Oswald Chambers*

Why I Wrote This Book

I BELIEVE THERE IS A NEW MODEL for how businesses must sell and service their local markets. This new model or business theory is crucial, whether you are a one-store operation or a 2,000-unit operation. Although the focus here is on business, the same principles and practices apply to government, religious organizations, or any other public sector entity that is faced with the challenge of serving highly diverse customer groups. These organizations rely on local delivery units — stores, branches, centers, churches, schools, or offices — with limited resources to respond to the varied needs, wants, and preferences of the local trade area. These differences may be a function of age, wealth, ethnicity, lifestyle, profession, marital status, sex, or any number of factors. For business-to-business applications, the factors may include geography, industry, size, operating philosophy, and corporate structure. But the bottom line is that customer groups in each local trade area or target market make very different demands on our sales-and-service delivery units.

And that is only half the challenge. In meeting these unique needs, businesses must deliver local sales and service in a more productive way. That means pressures to deliver value at the right cost: overdeliver, and we run the risk of being too expensive for the customer; underdeliver, and we risk providing less service than customers want. In most businesses, 80 percent of the customers are delivering less than 20 percent of the profits. If we are spending 80 percent of our time and resources on the 80 percent of the customers who contribute 20 percent of the profits, that is a productivity problem.

Most organizations have failed to respond to this productivity challenge with a strategy that tailors the sales and service of standard products to the unique needs of local target groups. To be competitive, they need a model that helps reengineer and reallocate their local resources to deliver the right sales, with the right service, to the right customer at the right cost. Although this challenge is greatest for companies that sell to thousands or even millions of individual consumers, companies that sell to other companies have also been limited in their ability to assess customer profitability and potential, implement lower-cost methods for managing low-value activities (e.g. paperwork, administration), and match sales-and-service costs to client needs.

The good news is that powerful technologies are becoming available to help companies achieve these productivity breakthroughs. Customers can be served by lower-cost, more responsive communication channels such as voice response units (VRUs), 1-800 numbers for 24-hour service access, and software for direct information access. Improved market information is available to help us evaluate local market preferences and potential. Enhanced customer information can help us assess customer profitability, potential, buying history, and patterns. These tools, provided by head office, offer great potential.

The bad news is that in most organizations, these corporate solutions are not integrated and managed in local branches, stores, and offices to optimize local productivity. Head office asks, "Why is the field so resistant to change?" Local managers ask, "Why does head office keep imposing solutions that do not fit my market?" Why? Because we have not provided the Streetcorner Strategy to apply them to the local market.

At the end of the day we run the risk of losing the battle in the local marketplace because we did not give customers what they wanted, and losing the productivity race because we overdelivered to some segments while underdelivering to others.

I believe there is a movement afoot to change all of this. In some respects this new movement is really a trip "back to the future," because it is what small-town grocers, banks, and hardware stores have always had to do — take special care of their best customers while serving a diverse local market. As always, the pressure for change comes from customers in local markets who are continually searching for alternatives that better meet their needs. To respond to this demand, sales-and-service delivery units must behave differently.

Because it seems so obvious and logical, many who are trying to respond to these market needs fail to understand fully the magnitude of reengineering and change required: analysis of local market potential, different service levels for different target groups, alternative delivery channels, local competitive differentiation, reallocation of sales-and-service resources, local market autonomy. These are significant changes; they require new processes, tools, practices, and — most of all — new learning. The discipline needed for local market mastery is no less than that for total quality management or time-based competition. No matter how noble the intention, how world-class the tactics, the ultimate challenge in more effectively managing local markets is managing cultural change.

My company, ActionSystems, has spent the past five years specifically researching local market management. We have helped analyze, develop, and implement plans for well over 2,000 local trade areas throughout North America. We believe there is now a body of knowledge that is quite instructive in understanding why the need for local market management is so urgent, what the crucial principles and practices are, and how companies can install the change. *The Streetcorner Strategy for Winning Local Markets* summarizes that body of knowledge: why to, what to, how to.

Who the Book Is For

The Streetcorner Strategy is for anyone who is interested in making local units more responsive and more productive:

- *Large company executives or small business owners* who are trying to invent a more effective sales-and-service distribution system, one that will grow *target* market share, lower the cost of selling and serving certain target groups, enhance the quality for others, and improve overall productivity.
- *Frontline sales-and-service staff* who arrive home each night stressed out from the never-ending challenge for more sales, better service, and more focus, but with less time and staff.
- *The marketing group* that is trying to get local units to use demographic, profitability, competitive, and other kinds of information to wage the local streetcorner-by-streetcorner battle more effectively.
- *Product managers* who are trying to get local units to focus on the best targets for their products in each local market.
- *Support functions* that are focused on service quality and are taking on the challenge to provide better service at less cost.

- *Those responsible for installing a sales culture* who are dealing with local units that lack clear-cut customer retention, growth, attraction, and cost strategies focused on identified target groups.

- *The financial staff* faced with lowering the cost of sales-and-service delivery while improving productivity.

- *Those who perform behind the scenes,* who do not have direct customer contact but who process, administer, and provide other forms of support, and who constantly grapple with the tradeoffs between lowest cost and flexible delivery.

- *The human resource group* that aids in selecting, training, incenting, and appraising — especially those in training and organizational development who help manage the learning for organization change.

This book presents the strategies for transforming the distribution-and-delivery side of the business. Ultimately, it is for anyone in an organization whose culture is moving with intention and purpose to become truly market driven. It is my hope that *The Streetcorner Strategy* can serve as a source of common vision, vocabulary, and practices for all who take up this charge.

Benefits to You, the Reader

ActionSystems' five years of research and experience have validated that there are opportunities for achieving breakthrough performance at the local market level — 20 percent to 30 percent profit improvement — by sizing potential, reengineering delivery, reallocating resources, and targeting the right segments proactively. Although head-office direction and support are imperative, making the breakthrough depends on the ability and commitment of the local team to develop and implement the Streetcorner Strategy for winning local markets.

Regardless of whether you are an executive running a large sales-and-service delivery organization, a store manager or small-business owner focused on a single trade area, or a front-line sales/service provider, you are feeling the pressure to perform at a higher, perhaps breakthrough, level. Your likely response to this pressure is simply to work harder. Hard work will be required, but it will not be enough. The answer is to shift gears. Our first mission in this book is to describe what things look like when you are running in the next gear. This means you must first look beneath the pain of your current condition and examine the limitations of how you are currently doing business — how it precludes your breakthrough.

Second, *The Streetcorner Strategy* describes how you operate when you shift into that next gear — a model for local market management and a road map for installing that model. It means that in order to break through to the next level, you must first change your thinking and, ultimately, your behavior. The payoff? Productivity up, profits up, customers up, employees up, and stress down.

Book Overview

The Streetcorner Strategy is organized in four parts:

Part I: Franchise at Risk

This first part describes the current symptoms of an old business model that is failing in industry after industry.

Part II: Defining the Real Problem

Part II describes how most organizations have treated the symptoms by stacking one fragmented solution atop another — in a series of waves — without stopping to address the cause or assess the risks of this approach in today's competitive environment. Part II concludes with a new way of managing these risks and avoiding the wave mentality.

Part III: The Breakout Performer

This part lays out three key principles that serve as a foundation for local market management.

Part IV: Market Driven

Part IV provides a road map of how to install the change. It deals specifically with the change process, the building blocks, the practices, the obstacles, and the *will* to make local market management work.

It is my hope and belief that this book will give expression to the truth that has been struggling in you for utterance.

PART

I

FRANCHISE AT RISK

*When the Old Ways
Don't Work Anymore*

*T*he airlines did it to the railroads. Foreign automobile manufacturers did it to U.S. car makers. Wal-Mart did it to Sears. Compaq did it to IBM and then Dell did it to Compaq. The nonbanks are doing it to the banks. Time after time we see established businesses discovering that the old way of doing things, successful for years, has become obsolete overnight. An enterprising competitor discovers or invents a faster, cheaper, or better way of responding to the needs and desires of a client; management fails to detect the trend in time or to respond quickly and forcefully to the change in the marketplace. Profitable revenue goes down, fixed costs remain fixed, margins slip, and managers discover that they have become stewards of a business in decline.

Until now, most of the emphasis has been on lowering the manufacturing cost and raising the quality of produced goods. Today, however, many companies find that they are hitting the wall with their sales and service. The process of selecting, creating, retaining, and growing customers in a local market is serious business, and it requires a large investment of resources. But many companies have sales-and-service delivery systems that cost too much and deliver too little — systems that fail, market by market, to productively tailor the delivery of standard products and services to the needs, opportunities, and potential in the local trade area.

The pain is especially acute in banks, retailing, airlines, and other service businesses that are under assault by highly focused competitors who have discovered weak links in their value chain — places where they are too expensive or where they underdeliver to customers who want better or different sales and service. And whether they are large, established sales-and-service delivery systems or small, mom-and-pop operations, their franchise — the current and future value of their enterprise — is at risk.

Like others that have suffered dramatic declines in times past, today's companies are debating the appropriate customer and market management response: should they improve service, or focus on sales, or lower costs, or become discounters, or do something else entirely? This debate is healthy; but many of these imperiled businesses will discover that failure to respond quickly with new ways of doing business can be lethal. In each major demise in American industry, the common characteristic has been the unwillingness of top management to acknowledge the danger and make the changes that must be made if the company is to survive and prosper.

In chapter 1 we will look at a number of companies and industries that are at risk because their sales-and-service delivery systems are losing steam. Then, in chapter 2, we will examine the key tenets of the old business model that is at the heart of the risk.

1

Hitting the Wall

The New Competitive Challenge

66 It ain't what people don't know that hurts, it's the things they know that ain't so. **99**[1]

— *Herbert Stein*

*I*S THERE REALLY A SALES-AND-SERVICE PROBLEM? Of course, every company has day-to-day problems satisfying individual customers, and any sales-and-service distribution system can be improved. But are these problems fundamental? Do they affect whole companies, entire industries? Our established companies built decades of success upon sales-and-service organizations that persuaded millions of customers to buy their products and come back for more. Has the game suddenly changed? Have we really hit the wall?

Ask department stores. Many have idle clerks waiting around to serve customers who have gone to the discount stores. Why? Because these customers saw little value in paying 10 to 20 percent more for a sales clerk whose idea of adding value was to ask, "May I help you?"

Wal-Mart, as the quintessential discounter, went from $0 to $40 billion in revenue in 29 years. They invented no new products, nor a store environment that couldn't be duplicated. But they did *something*, because they average better than 50 percent more revenue per square foot than their competitors: they targeted their markets differently.[2] They started out in communities large enough for one discount store but not large enough for two. They figured out how to deliver merchandise, sell to customers, and provide service at a lower price than local merchants. Although they gained great economies of scale in purchasing and distribution, they also mastered Sam Walton's first principle of retailing: "Think one store at a time."[3] As they grew, they focused on "acting small" in the local market.

At the other end of the price continuum, Nordstrom has gained recognition for its sales-and-service culture (with some mixed reviews). For a while it seemed as if every company on the continent had set its sights on being the Nordstrom of service in its industry. What many companies failed to recognize was that Nordstrom's sales-and-service strategy worked for them because it targeted a market willing to pay for world-class sales and service in both price and repeat business.

The economics of Nordstrom's service quality do not work across all market segments — and even Nordstrom is now struggling to stay profitable while competing with other retailers whose selling costs are lower. High service quality without high repeat business, volume, or margins may just be highly unprofitable. Bloomingdale's, Sears, and Macy's are all struggling with the challenge of successfully aligning their sales, service, and costs.

Some automobile dealers saw significant increases in local car sales after they got rid of their sales force. Why? Because buying a car was a hassle. Eliminating the hassle of dealing with the local salesperson added value while lowering cost. The number of salespeople in American industry goes down each year because there are less expensive and more efficient ways to fill orders. A salesperson must bring to the job more than the ability to fill an order; he or she must help identify needs, offer alternatives, and provide information that can lead local customers to better decisions.

The airlines face a similar challenge. They have spent years expanding their hub-and-spoke system while upgrading their services: special meals, frequent-flier programs, reserved seating. However, somewhere along the way something happened (table 1.1).

American Airlines, recognized as the top service airline in the industry by the American Aviation Association, has questioned the

Rank	1990	1991	1992
1	American	American	American
2	Delta	Southwest	Southwest
3	Southwest	Delta	United
4	United	United	Delta
5	USAir	USAir	USAir
6	Pan Am	Pan Am	Northwest
7	Northwest	Northwest	America West
8	Continental	Continental	Continental
9	TWA	America West	TWA
10	America West	TWA	—

Brent D. Bowen, University of Nebraska at Omaha; Dean E. Headley, Wichita State University; adapted from The Dallas Morning News, *April 13, 1993, p. 1A.*

Table 1.1. Airline Quality Survey

success of its own service quality. Chairman Robert L. Crandall signaled that the game had changed when he stated:

> Customers clearly said a simpler product at a lower price is better.... [The company] cannot impose on itself or on its customers the costs of product features they don't want.[4]

Much of the pressure that Crandall describes is created by a smaller regional carrier, Southwest Airlines, which flies many of the same routes, serves no meals, reserves no seats, and follows a credo that says airlines make money flying — not on the ground. Compared to the major airlines that average 30 to 45 minutes on the ground between landing and takeoff, Southwest averages ten to fifteen minutes. If you choose, you can purchase your ticket at an airport ticket machine with a credit card, which is very convenient and efficient for both the company and the passenger.

While American Airlines lost nearly $1 billion in 1992, Southwest Airlines, with its lower costs and lower fares, has become a breakout performer by reengineering the way it targets its market and delivers sales and service. Major airlines that have been successful for decades are now asking whether they can survive in this new environment (table 1.2).

One of the leaders in the convenience-store industry, 7-Eleven Food Stores closed 358 stores in 1992 while opening just 34 new ones.

Statistic	Southwest	American*
Net profits per employee	$2,753	–$2,068
Operating profits per employee	$6,436	$192
Passengers per employee	2,318	835
Employees per aircraft	79	146
Available seat miles per employee	1,891,082	1,466,725
Revenue passenger miles per employee	1,155,265	904,780

*Net income figures for American are for its parent, AMR Corp. Available seat miles translates into one seat flown one mile. Revenue passenger miles is based on one paying passenger flown one mile.

AMR Corp., Southwest Airlines Co.; adapted from The Dallas Morning News, February 16, 1992

Table 1.2. Airline Productivity: American vs. Southwest, 1991

Recognizing the need to change their system at the local store level, they are giving more responsibility to store managers for purchasing and managing inventories to fit local customer tastes. The company will continue to close more stores than it opens each year. Ralt Bohn, one of 7-Eleven's divisional general managers, explains:

> In the past, it had been how many locations can you build and how much stuff can you sell. That is changing as the convenience store industry is changing. The practice of putting stuff up, stacking it high and letting it fly is over.[5]

And in Japan, 7-Eleven has taken this change to the next level. Using point-of-sale cash registers, they feed data directly to powerful computers. Sales clerks even key in each customer's sex and estimated age. With this system, storekeepers can identify their best customers and keep track of what and when they like to buy.[6]

The traditional model of expansion and growth has been tested, and the old assumptions found wanting.

A CASE STUDY

A MORE IN-DEPTH EXAMPLE helps illustrate the point. Let's look at the brokerage firms and mutual fund companies and how they have mauled the banks. In 1982, bank customers had $1.18 trillion (80 percent) in certificates of deposit (CDs), compared with $297 billion (20 percent) in mutual funds. In March 1992, for the first time in history, mutual funds exceeded CDs (table 1.3). Much of that money (experts estimate 70 to 85 percent) moved from banks to mutual funds and brokerage firms. That is a major setback for banks.

However, the scary part is that banks will find it difficult to get the money back when mutual funds fall out of favor. Even more disturbing, this erosion is occurring with the banks' most profitable customers — the 10 to 15 percent who contribute more than 75 percent of the profits. The clincher is that while the banks' highly profitable balances moved to the mutual funds and brokerage firms, their costly transaction business stayed with them. Some brokerage firms

Period	Mutual Funds*	Certificates of Deposit*
1982	$ 296.7	$ 1,179.8
1983	292.9	1,113.0
1984	370.7	1,306.7
1985	495.5	1,321.5
1986	716.3	1,295.3
1987	769.9	1,405.8
1988	810.3	1,572.0
1989	982.0	1,704.6
1990	1,066.9	1,662.1
1991	1,348.2	1,501.0
1992	1,595.4	1,223.0
1993 (September)	1,913.2	1,138.7

* billions of dollars   *Adapted from Investment Company Institute, Federal Reserve*

Table 1.3. Banks Lose Market Share

now charge customers a fee to close out their accounts. Their retention strategy acknowledges the real cost of closing out an account
and puts a "tax" on leaving. The banks' formerly profitable A (most
profitable) customers become C (least profitable) customers overnight, and their most valuable business will be hard to get back.

Banks are not losing this business in head-to-head "bake-offs"
for customers. As Woody Allen said, "Showing up is 80 percent of
life."[7] The banks are just not "showing up." Why? Because they are
so busy responding to their "demand" customers that there is no
time to proactively go after their best customers who seldom come to
the branch. Highly effective sales and distribution systems show up
"on purpose" — that is, with the right customers.

THINGS COULD GET WORSE

AS HIGH-COST PROVIDERS with bricks and mortar on every corner,
banks have lost their most profitable business to lower-cost providers
while retaining their unprofitable transaction business. As a dis-

proportionate amount of their business is transactional, costs go up, service goes down, attention to the best customers is diminished, and prospecting efforts decrease. A senior executive of one of the largest retail branch systems in North America recently said, "We are going to become the farm club for the major leagues if we don't get back in the game on these deposit balances."

The problem is much larger than just deposits. In 1987, banks had 80 percent of the credit card business; this has now fallen to 62 percent. In 1987, they had 37 percent of the assets for defined-contribution retirement plans; now they have 31 percent. While demand has been flat or declining for small-business and commercial loans, Merrill Lynch and Company reports a 70 percent increase in its financing business.[8] While banks have been closing and consolidating branches, the number of check-cashing installations by nonbanks has nearly tripled since 1987 from 1,538 to 4,125 locations.[9] In addition, these check cashiers, with their lower-cost delivery systems, are moving upmarket and offering additional services, including money transfers, money orders, traveler's checks, utility bill payments, photocopying, and facsimiles. There are other examples, including dealer automobile financing, corporate lending — the list goes on. In fact, consultant Bert Ely calculates that since 1978 banks have lost 42 percent of their market share to mutual funds, finance companies, insurers, and other lenders.[10]

It is no exaggeration to say that the banking industry is under attack. The current rate environment, regulation, recession, mergers, and a growing financial services industry have all served to mask a core problem. Banks are being dramatically outsold by nonbanks. They are not losing many customers, but they are losing a ton of their customers' business — they are losing share of wallet (fig. 1.1).

$$\text{Share of wallet} = \frac{\text{Customer's total expenditure with us}}{\text{Customer's total expenditure with all providers}}$$

Figure 1.1. Share of Wallet

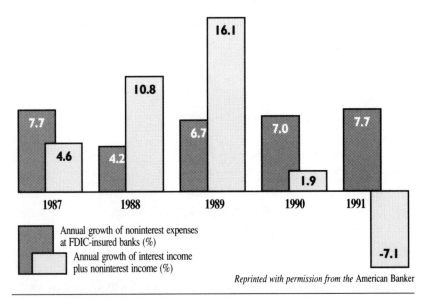

Annual growth of noninterest expenses at FDIC-insured banks (%)
Annual growth of interest income plus noninterest income (%)

Reprinted with permission from the American Banker

Figure 1.2. Bank Expenses Rise, Revenue Growth Lags

The expense side of the picture is also a problem. In spite of all the talk about expense reduction, since 1987 the annual growth of noninterest expenses, such as the cost of employees and overhead, has not gone down, according to the Federal Deposit Insurance Corporation (FDIC). As seen in figure 1.2, revenue growth has declined, and revenue actually shrank in 1991.[11] When we compare the banks to their nonbank competitors, it looks even worse (fig. 1.3).[12] The bank's sales-and-service delivery system costs about four times as much as its most efficient nonbank competitors per dollar of loans and deposits. Rising expenses, shrinking revenue, and dramatic loss of market share, particularly in the high-profit segments, are a deadly combination.

If things are so bad, why are current bank earnings so respectable? There are two reasons. First, the overall growth of the financial services industry has allowed year-to-year revenue growth to continue in many cases — even if it is at a slower rate. In other words, the pie is getting larger even if the banks' slice isn't. Second, unusually wide net-interest margins camouflage the significant loss of

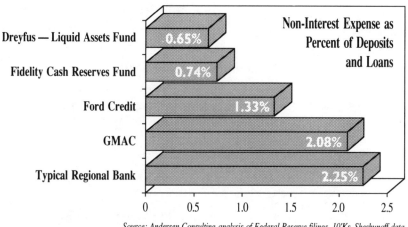

Source: Andersen Consulting analysis of Federal Reserve filings, 10'Ks, Sheshunoff data

Figure 1.3. Banks vs. Nonbanks

earning potential and market share. It is especially tempting to ignore the early warning signals of customer retention problems as long as revenue is growing and profits are adequate.

IT'S NOT JUST BANKS

WE DON'T HAVE TO LOOK FAR to see what happens to an industry when it loses large chunks of market share, especially when it is a higher-cost producer. The "Big Three" automobile manufacturers were attacked by Mercedes-Benz and BMW on the upper end of the market, and by Volkswagen and Honda on the lower end. Before it was over, all segments were under attack. Competitors started by differentiating on quality in the upper end and price in the lower end, and they won both battles while expanding to the middle.

That is exactly what happens to a market leader when niche players come in and take away its most profitable customers. Product sales may hold up for a while, but usually when businesses experience customer retention problems, they are silently trading profitable customers for less profitable or even unprofitable ones.

Eventually revenue goes down while costs remain high; in some businesses, costs even go up. For example, in the grocery industry, if customers who average 20 items per checkout are traded for customers who are averaging eight, checkout labor costs will go up. Even if enough new customers are attracted to make up for the volume lost, costs are significantly increased and profits are lowered.

IT'S NOT JUST THE BIG GUYS

LET'S LOOK AT A SMALL BUSINESS. The folks who run my favorite bookstore are near and dear to me, and I am really quite satisfied with them. However, I wonder how satisfied they would be with me if they knew the whole story about our relationship.

I wonder, for example, if they know that I have bought about 50 books from them in the past four years. Do they know that virtually all of my purchases have been business books? Are they aware that I have bought another 15 or so books elsewhere, at airports, malls, etc., because I just happened to see a title that interested me? So at an average of $25 a book, they have received $1,250 in revenue from me, but missed $375 that I would gladly have spent with them if they had brought the same titles to my attention. They got over 75 percent of my wallet; how might they have gotten it all, and more?

Well, they might have identified and targeted me as one of their business-book segment customers. They might have sent me a quarterly listing of their newly released business titles. The Tattered Cover, a great bookstore in Denver, has a large business-book section and sends its segment customers a quarterly newsletter featuring many of the new releases. That means they get "shelf space" in the mind, regardless of whether customers are coming into the store. If my bookstore sent me such a list, I might buy another four books a year — another $100 in annual revenue for them.

If they were to analyze my buying pattern, they would find that more than half of my purchases were made on Saturdays, between 6:30 p.m. and 7:15 p.m. Perhaps they would discern the reason for this pattern: my wife and I like to attend movies in that small strip mall. In effect, the qualities and types of these movies affect the quantity and makeup of their store traffic.

What is also very relevant is that my wife buys about two books a month, and my two daughters average three books a month between them. They tend to buy more paperbacks and are less interested in new releases than I am. More price conscious than I, they buy most of their books from a discount store. At an average price of $7.50 per book, they spend $37.50 a month, or $450 a year.

So the good news is that I like my corner bookstore and buy there when I can. The service is good, the selection is good, and it is a convenient, fun visit, particularly in conjunction with a movie.

The bad news is that they are working off an old business model. They are managing the store, not the market. They are segmented in their store layout (sections for business books, children's books, etc.) but not in their management of customers. They are proactive in helping you find books, but not in helping you buy what you want when you don't have time to visit the store.

This past year they captured $300 of my business but lost $100 to other stores and missed perhaps another $100 because I didn't come to the store frequently enough. Of the $850 our household spent on books last year, they let $550 get away. They got less than 36 percent of our total wallet.

The plot thickens. A new, large, discount bookstore is being built less than half a mile from them. If it has a large business section, targets newsletters to that segment, and offers a low price — what happens? The $300 that they could expect to get from me next year now becomes at risk. They will do fine without my $300, but if business-book buyers are a significant segment for them, a 20 percent or 30 percent defection rate could cause them great pain.

Department stores, airlines, and other business segments are under the same pressures. How does an industry or a company or a local store fail to respond to this level of competitive encroachment? As the editorial page of *The Wall Street Journal* stated it:

There was a moment when Detroit recognized that Americans were beginning to buy large numbers of foreign-made cars, when IBM noticed that its industry was moving away from large mainframe computers, when Sears saw its first Wal-Mart, when Big Steel saw its product turn into a commodity. The time for decisions was then. They waited until later. Too late.[13]

Many companies today are hitting the wall. Complex and interrelated challenges lie behind these struggles. One of those challenges is the need for sales-and-service distribution systems to perform at a higher level.

Our purpose here is to focus on that challenge — how to transform sales-and-service delivery into a highly productive, responsive system. As most businesses and industries mature, the importance of local sales and service becomes more and more crucial to success. The ability of these units to tailor the delivery of standard products and services, which may have become commodity items, to the needs of the local market will often be the single most important predictor of success.

In order to move beyond a simplistic description of the pain, we must understand some of the root causes of the sales-and-service distribution problem. That is the topic of our next chapter.

2

The Old Business Model

A Sure Bet for Losing Your Franchise

66 Insanity is continuing to do the same things and hoping to get different results. **99**

— Author unknown

Y ES, THERE IS A PROBLEM. Many of our sales-and-service distribution systems are underperforming. Why? What are the root causes?

First of all, the world has changed and so has the marketplace. A quiet revolution is occurring in how and where customers are choosing to buy. This revolution is bringing with it a new standard for how effective sales-and-service delivery systems must perform. Given today's emerging technology, face-to-face buying is now optional in many industries — customers do it only if it makes sense. Today's banks, department stores, and other retailers are struggling to get their best customers to come in. Yankelovich Partners, a market research firm, found in a 1992 survey that the number of shoppers who enjoyed buying clothes fell from 40 percent in 1989 to 31 percent in 1992.[1] Banks see less of their best customers each year.

Personalized service is optional. Customers will decide whether they prefer doing business face to face or by phone, mail, satellite, computer, or machine interface. These delivery mechanisms have very different costs, levels of convenience, and value to customers. Although businesses will have to decide corporately the diverse channels on which they are willing to bet, local trade areas vary greatly in their needs and preferences. For example, an automatic teller machine (ATM) transaction costs a bank about a third as much as the same transaction face to face. Nonetheless, in predominantly senior-citizen markets usage will not be high, because this group is often averse to technology and enjoys the social interaction of visiting a branch.

It is interesting that many companies are spending millions on research to decide which channels to select, but little or nothing to prepare and train local managers to assess, target, and tailor these distribution channels to their unique local markets. When the crunch comes, these sales-and-service units will be untargeted in their sales, untailored in their service, and inefficient in their use of local alternative channels of distribution. They will spend too much time delivering the basics and will lack sufficient resources to add value and sell to their high-potential customers. They will look too expensive.

A more precise definition of the problem is poor sales-and-service productivity — which leads us to a critical question: How much of our revenue is created by our distribution system?

WHAT ARE WE REALLY BETTING ON?

WHAT HAVE BUSINESSES DONE TO RESPOND to this changing world? Not enough. Peter Drucker says that many companies and industries in decline need to invent a new business theory to fit current and future reality.[2] When we look beyond the jargon of many sales-and-service distribution systems, we see tired practices based on an old business theory. The world has changed but we haven't. No one would dare to describe his or her own strategy this way, but in people's actual skills, behaviors, and practices for sales and service in local markets, we see six flawed assumptions that are products of the old business model.

Flawed assumption 1: One size fits all. The first assumption is that we can use one standard approach to serve all customers and markets. When it comes to designing products, we have acknowledged that customers have different needs, but we have been much slower in designing different sales, service, and delivery mechanisms. Grocery chains were slow in responding to the increased need for speed and convenience — hence, the growth of the convenience-store industry. Banks, hampered by regulation, were slow to provide consultation and investment services to their more sophisticated branch customers — thus, dramatic gains by brokerage firms and mutual funds companies in selling investment products and services, which represent approximately 30 percent loss of market share for the banks.

In spite of extensive research on customer satisfaction, the automobile industry has been slow to recognize that most of their customers do not enjoy "horse trading" or the automobile version of "Let's Make a Deal." It is interesting that an industry that was a leader in product segmentation to meet varying customer needs —

for example, General Motors' Chevrolet, Pontiac, Oldsmobile, Buick, and Cadillac divisions — has been oblivious to the same needs in sales and service. Similarly, the airlines that invented first-class, business-class, and coach service are struggling to compete with the regional airlines that have reengineered their approach to sales and service.

So often, we *have* designed segmented delivery mechanisms, but we have done it according to an old business theory that no longer fits current reality. For example, when we talk with bankers about segmentation, they often say that they offer commercial, private, and retail banking. Unfortunately, huge chunks of customer wallet fall through those cracks. It is the mission of the local delivery unit to take standard products and services and tailor sales-and-service capabilities to meet the unique needs of the local market.

Flawed assumption 2: History is the best guide to market potential. Everyone knows that market potential varies greatly across trade areas. Yet very often, goals are set by executives several levels above the market manager — too far removed to understand the market potential. This places too much emphasis on peer comparison or history. In some local markets, a 15 percent improvement over the previous year may be well below potential, while in others, where the market is shrinking, a zero percent increase may be outstanding. By ignoring these factors, we tend to miss opportunities to tailor our management of growth areas and flat or shrinking markets. In addition, we often cut costs across the board, mistakenly assuming that cutting each market the same amount will have the same impact and results.

Flawed assumption 3: Head office knows best. How often have we seen head office use the same promotion to paint the whole market-place, assuming that it would be successful in every local trade area? How many times have we seen local market managers object to the promotion as a poor fit for their local market? How much time, energy, and executive credibility have been sacrificed to force compliance? How many market managers have given up and are just going through the motions to appease the boss? How much time of local staff have been wasted working on a campaign that makes no sense in their area? The same efforts and initiatives will not create the same results; everyone knows it, but the campaigns, promotions, and training blitzes roll on.

Flawed assumption 4: All revenue is good revenue. Pushing product revenue without considering customer needs, service costs, or customer retention can put the squeeze on profits even while expanding the business. We have had too many quality and service initiatives that increased revenue but raised costs even more. Quality and service may attract business, but they require investment.

Our company recently worked with a bank that had significant market share in one of its regions. The local management team decided that its best opportunity was to focus on high-deposit customers and try to improve penetration and gain a greater share of wallet. It also found that it was losing money on many of its low-end customers, so it decided to serve the ones it had and *not* try to attract additional accounts.

Unknown to the branch managers, one of the product managers ran a campaign across all regions advertising an attractive rate for opening new deposit accounts. The branches in the region were bombarded with new customers opening small-deposit accounts. They had to increase staffing, which drove up costs, and virtually abandon their calling effort on targeted high-deposit customers, who were particularly at risk to competing mutual funds and brokerage firms. The new customers proved to be rate sensitive and susceptible to newspaper advertising, and thus were likely to move their accounts across the street, at a closeout cost of $20 to $50 each, during the competitor's next rate special. Yes, volume went up — but so did costs, and so did the risk of losing valuable customers.

Flawed assumption 5: Your biggest competitors are your toughest competitors. Executives and managers often invest scarce resources studying the wrong competitors, with no mechanism to assess local competitors. Sears worried about Montgomery Ward, American Airlines worried about Delta, and large banks worried about other large banks. Usually, however, the war is fought in streetcorner battles. In mature markets with similar products, the real competition is the knowledge, skills, and commitment of the team across the street.

Senior management *should* worry about established competitors, but they should also be aware of the often greater threat from upstarts, like Dell Computer for IBM, Canon fax machines for Federal Express, and Wal-Mart for Sears. No matter how brilliant the head office's competitive analysis, most local market managers are up against a unique set of competitive circumstances. In many local markets, 50 to 60 percent of the competition is someone the head office doesn't know or care about.

Flawed assumption 6: Staff will respond enthusiastically to ideas that don't fit their market. We know this assumption is not true, yet we are often surprised at the depth of anger and resentment from people in the local market over decisions that just don't fit. Empowerment is the talk of the day, but when it comes to resource allocation (for example, productivity initiatives, process improvement, campaigns to pass up), it is illusory.

Many on the front lines are beyond anger; they have abdicated. Those who serve customers every day — who are closest to their wants and needs, who sit by them at ball games and at church — lack input and empowerment. We ask for these front-line troops to be warm, friendly, and productive, yet we seldom involve them in the engineering and design of local sales-and-service delivery.

At the core of these six flawed practices is the assumption that the head office knows best. Yet when you talk with most people in the head office, that is really not their belief. It is not so much that they think they know best as that they are struggling with how to make local market management work. Everyone knows that there are certain decisions and strategies that must come out of the corporate office: achieving economies of scale, strategic focus, product development, and brand identity, among others. The problem is how to find the balance between corporate and local interests and to apply corporate strategies by tailoring local tactics and practices.

So if everyone knows that we cannot run the company effectively from the head office, why aren't we doing a better job locally? As a colleague of mine once said, "If everyone knows the Ten Commandments, how come we still got sin?"

STRATEGIES "Я" US

ONE OF THE REASONS WE STRUGGLE with market management is that we are stuck in old ways of thinking and old ways of viewing the organization. We see strategy in terms of organizational functions. Despite all the talk about being organized around the customer, most companies are organized functionally: sales, service, product management, and marketing. This makes us very inefficient in developing and implementing customer-driven local market strategy.

Productivity and Customer Value

The problem we have on the customer side of the business is similar to that on the manufacturing side: low productivity. In most industries we manage all customers and markets as if they were the same. This is inefficient. Their needs are different, their willingness to pay is different, their cost of servicing is different, their profitability is different, and their potential is different. Most businesses derive more than 80 percent of their profits from 20 percent of their customers — yet many companies that serve retail and small business customers have not allocated time, effort, and value based on the potential contribution of local customers. Spending 80 percent of sales and service time on customers who generate less than 20 percent of the profits — that is a productivity problem.

"Fad-egy" vs. Strategy

Why are we struggling with these issues? Because we have substituted fads for strategy. Someone says the problem is sales, so we focus on sales. We establish incentives and conduct sales training and say, "Let's get some volume going," and sure enough, sales go up. A few months down the road someone says, "Well, we got so focused on sales that service went down. We weren't prepared for the volume and now we must fix service problems and stop the customer defections." So everyone gets focused on service, and we invest heavily in giving customers what they want. Then someone says, "It sure is getting expensive. We need to cut costs." So the long knives come out, and we say everyone must give a pint of blood. Then someone says, "Total quality management is the way to go," and everyone jumps on that bandwagon. (Disposable razors, disposable diapers, disposable strategies — has a certain ring, doesn't it?)

At the end of the day, we look like the gang who couldn't shoot straight, because there was no *market* strategy.

- We invested heavily in sales efforts to attract some new customers who are loss leaders, and lost some of our most profitable customers because we could not service them effectively.

- We invested heavily in service quality, which took our eye off sales and costs. In many cases, we also increased service levels to customers who were already getting more than they were paying for (loss leaders).

- We trimmed costs across the board. As a result, some of our best customers, wooed by the competition, felt they were getting less value (service) than they wanted or deserved — and left.

- We improved quality across all parts of our business. Unfortunately, because we did not target specific market segments, the improvement brought little value to some of our most important target groups, while increasing costs on some of our unprofitable customers.

STRATEGIC CONNECTIVITY

IF WE WERE ON THE MANAGEMENT INFORMATION SYSTEMS side of the business, we might define this dilemma as a *connectivity* problem.

This is the term that systems people use to describe hardware and software that won't connect to or run on other hardware or software. Sound familiar? Our sales strategy is not connected to our service strategy is not connected to our cost strategy. The results are strikingly similar to those experienced in the systems area:

- Constant reinvestment in hardware and software, with disappointing results.
- Discarding of expensive systems investments that quickly become obsolete.
- Frenzied initiatives to patch systems together.
- Inefficient use of computing capability.

A whole industry of systems integrators has emerged to deal with connectivity. The problem with poor strategic connectivity — the lack of coordination among various company strategies — is that people are less resilient than hardware and software. Thinking people get tired and frustrated when today's strategy and support systems (goals, information, rewards, training) don't connect or, even worse, contradict those that were so urgent yesterday. Connectivity problems occur when systems get built one at a time in response to a very specific set of needs, with little thought given to the overall information needs of the enterprise. Such an approach is transactional, short term, and reactive.

One of the crucial roles of market management is to integrate strategies for sales, service, quality, and cost, and to refocus and refine these issues to win and profit in local markets. To have strategic connectivity, we must step back and look at the whole delivery system from the customer's point of view. A customer service initiative that contradicts sales training, a cost reduction initiative that is mute on service quality, a Total Quality Management initiative that ignores market segments — each is a strategic connectivity problem. It may not show up as a single line item cost, but it is like trashing the reservation system for an airline, or the loan system for a bank, or the product cost system for a grocer. It is very expensive, and it takes a heavy toll in lost employee and customer currency.

Absent a strategic thrust, it is also addictive, because whatever part of the sales/service/cost/markets equation it neglects will become tomorrow's crisis, which will define the following day's initiative.

And it makes our people very tired. The cost in campaigns, initiatives, management time, and employee energy makes this approach to business management unproductive. This level of churn and burn undermines management and erodes the company's ability to do battle. The lack of integration of sales, service, quality, and cost strategies can lead to the disintegration of the company, because strategic gridlock in the corner office causes train wrecks in local stores or branches where markets are won or lost.

We must ask: What kinds of customers do we want? What types of service do they need? Where should we lower costs (which target groups)? What quality enhancements will bring value? When we do not ask these crucial questions, we fail to get the results we want. Running a local market means aligning sales, service, quality, and cost simultaneously to meet the needs of and deliver value to *target groups* (homogeneous customer or prospect groups having similar buying motives within a *market segment* — a portion of the local market characterized by its actual or potential profit or revenue contribution to the company). Getting one of them right while ignoring the others will almost always be wrong. Local market management requires a more comprehensive, strategic approach to looking at the market both globally and locally. And it means delivering different levels of sales, service, and quality to different target groups, sometimes out of the same delivery unit, based on their needs and willingness to pay.

FIGHTING IT OUT, STREETCORNER BY STREETCORNER

THE REAL BATTLEGROUND IS THE LOCAL MARKET. For service-oriented businesses with similar products, 70 to 80 percent of what is important is determined locally — and virtually all businesses are ultimately service businesses. Friendliness, productivity, product knowledge, convenience, flexibility, hours, staff competence — these are local market issues. The objective is a sales-and-service delivery system that profitably delivers value relative to the needs of local customers and prospects. That means doing *some* things differently from one market to another — things that can add value. It also means lowering the cost of delivering to some customers, because price matters.

Zeroing In on Customers

The unit around which we organize our efforts is not the product, it is the customer. We must know which customers to build a fence around; which ones are high potential, warranting a move-up or penetration strategy; which customer groups are too costly to serve; and which prospects we must attract if we are to build the value of the local franchise.

The energy source for winning the local market is local teams empowered, skilled, and accountable for profitably winning the local market. Their primary mission is not compliance to head office, but a commitment to do whatever it takes to be the provider of choice for the target groups they have focused on locally.

CREATING LOCAL MARKET "HEATSEEKERS"

EVERYONE NOW TALKS OF MARKET-DRIVEN, empowered teams commissioned to win their local markets, but most companies lack a business theory or a model for making it happen, operating instead off an old model that gets in the way. This old model is so constraining that only the strongest 5 to 10 percent of managers can force the necessary changes and throw off the shackles. These mavericks, often our best performers, have invented a local market management theory that works for them. But the rest are not strong enough to invent a local market approach to doing business.

This is backward. We should be providing our sales-and-service distribution system with a better model — a model that includes the principles, processes, practices, skills, and tools that will bring success for 80 to 90 percent of these managers in their local markets. However, without such a model, without local managers who possess the necessary principles and skills, executive management is probably wise to control and constrain, for it is *enablement* that allows *empowerment* to pay off. A lot of executives know in their heart of hearts that their people have not been given the knowledge and resources to run the local show. They know that this lack of understanding can lead to some really dumb local decisions. So they have hit the wall. They are stuck — executives and local managers alike — in an old business model that sub-optimizes performance, because they have not designed a system for *empowerment* at the local market.

This book focuses on how to profitably win the local market — streetcorner by streetcorner — by delivering value tailored to the needs of local customers and prospects. The objective is to create "heatseekers" — local teams and individuals who identify, select, seek, and develop the optimum mix of customers and prospects available in a local market.

Our assumption is simple: The way to optimize the contribution of the sales-and-service distribution system to the company is to optimize the available potential in each local trade area. Conversely, a sure way to sub-optimize the return to the business is to sub-optimize in each local trade area. We will use the term *local market management* to describe a set of practices — the Streetcorner Strategy — that maximizes the value to local customers and prospects, value to employees, and value to shareholders by profitably winning the local market.

The tenets of local market management via the Streetcorner Strategy are common sense, but seldom are they common practice. The jargon is familiar: market segmentation; local market empowerment; differentiated service delivery; customer-driven, value-added service; low-cost provider; total quality management. And that's the problem. How do all these tenets tie together? Some seem to contradict others. Which get driven centrally? Which are driven locally? For those that are driven centrally, how do we align ourselves, and how much latitude do we have, to apply them locally? To profitably win our local markets without creating chaos requires us to knit the answers together into a single fabric.

It is important to point out that local market management does not mean that each local manager does as he or she pleases. In fact, the clearer head office can be about strategy, market segments, and financial performance expectations, the easier it is to focus effectively in the local trade area. While these central strategic issues are a crucial part of success, our focus in this book will be on how to apply them locally.

The remaining chapters of this book define the paradigm shift, the principles, the cultural change, and the practices required to successfully install the Streetcorner Strategy. Ultimately, what we are seeking is a new skill set for sales-and-service distribution organizations that are committed to breakout performance — streetcorner by streetcorner.

II

DEFINING
THE
REAL
PROBLEM

The Risks of the
"Program of the Month"
Mentality

We have all experienced the wave. You were at the stadium or saw it on television. People in one part of the stadium stand up, wave and yell, and just as they start to sit down, the next group stands, waves, yells, and then sits down. As the wave moves around the stadium, it gains momentum, and may even circle the stadium seven or eight times before it dies.

If we think of the wave as a metaphor for corporate initiatives, we can readily see some parallels to the "program of the month" syndrome that has hit many companies, perhaps even our own. First, there was the sales wave. Everyone focused on getting a sales culture, and when it came our time, we stood up, waved our arms, and yelled. And we watched that wave work its way through the company.

About the time the sales wave was getting to the front line, a new wave emerged. Proponents of the new wave said that it wasn't really sales but service quality that was most important. Customer retention, Malcolm Baldrige, and Total Quality Management (TQM) were the real watchwords for the organization. Once again, when it came our turn, we stood, waved and yelled, with ever-so-slightly less enthusiasm.

Again we watched as the movement made its rounds through the company. We also observed some people's puzzlement and frustration. What about the sales culture wave? How did it fit with service? The waving and yelling were so intense, however, that these questions were not heard or addressed.

And just as the service wave was completing its circuit, yet another wave began — "less cost." Target staffing, right sizing, branch or store rationalization, and low-cost producer were the new watchwords. As this ripple started through the company, it became noticeable that some people stood, waved, and yelled without enthusiasm. A few arguments broke out about the merits of the service wave over those of the cost wave. It took on the feeling of the old Miller Lite beer commercials: "Tastes great!" "Less filling!" And as this last wave lumbered through the crowd, a new unanimity emerged: Before we do any more waves, let's determine how these last three fit together.

In the Southwest United States there is a phrase describing care of horses that takes me back to my childhood growing up on a ranch: "rode hard and put up wet." It refers to extracting maximum effort from the animal and then not drying it off before the coolness of the night sets in, increasing the likelihood of pneumonia. Many employees feel the same way. They are not up for another series of quarter-mile races.

If we are to bring coherence to this chaos, we must go back and understand each wave and try to see how it all ties together. The next two chapters will look at these waves — with their emphasis on sales, service, and cost — to understand the driving force behind each one and the limitations on productivity and customer value associated with them. The final two chapters of this part will identify the risks this wave mentality creates for the business enterprise and propose an integrated model for removing this risk by reengineering sales, service, and costs. Understanding these limitations and risks is crucial if we are to know what we must change as we move sales and service into a more productive, customer-driven mode — profitably winning local markets.

3

The Sales Wave

Stand Up if the Problem Is Not Enough Revenue

❝ My dad gave me one dollar bill
'Cause I'm his smartest son,
And I swapped it for two shiny quarters
'Cause two is more than one! ...

... And then I took the quarters
And traded them to Lou
For three dimes — I guess he don't know
That three is more than two!

Just then, along came old blind Bates
And just 'cause he can't see
He gave me four nickels for my three dimes
And four is more than three!

And I took the nickels to Hiram Coombs
Down at the seed-feed store,
And the fool gave me five pennies for them,
And five is more than four!

And then I went and showed my dad,
And he got red in the cheeks
And closed his eyes and shook his head —
Too proud of me to speak![1]

— Shel Silverstein

"Smart," *from* Where the Sidewalk Ends, *by Shel Silverstein. ©1974 by Evil Eye Music, Inc. Reprinted by permission of HarperCollins Publishers.*

*F*OR MOST COMPANIES THE MAIN OBJECTIVE of the sales organization has been to produce revenue. The assumption by and large has been that all revenue is the same. Fear of too little revenue, loss of market share, lack of distribution capacity, and the resultant loss to the competition has led to the conventional wisdom that you could never have too much revenue, too many customers, or too large a distribution system.

Yet those very assumptions have lead to some very high-cost, underperforming customer sales-and-service delivery systems with a limited ability to meet highly diverse customer needs. Not surprisingly, these challenges have led companies to reevaluate the productivity and value created by their sales and service.

Paul Carroll, a *Wall Street Journal* reporter, described the dilemma of John Akers before he stepped down as CEO at IBM:

He recognized that IBM's vaunted sales force had become an enormous expense and put in place a plan to turn IBM salesmen into consultants who would bill customers for their time. Unfortunately, the plan called for doing that with 5 percent of the salesmen a year, meaning the shift would take 20 years. Former executives say that those salesmen who can't make it as consultants need to go. They say, more than half seriously, that routine mainframe sales, like PC sales, would be done through mail order.[2]

How quickly things change. What was just a few years earlier the most revered sales organization in the world became almost overnight a fading CEO's ball and chain.

This chapter examines four critical phases of evolution for sales-and-service distribution systems as they move to a market-driven sales culture. Although a number of progressive companies began building a strong sales culture much earlier, others did not start until the late 1970s and early 1980s. However, even some of the progressive companies became stuck before completing the transition. We will examine each of the phases and look at how productivity and customer value ultimately emerge as the crucial outcomes. In the process, we will describe the paradigm shift that sales organizations must embrace to win the battle, a streetcorner at at time.

PHASE 1: WHEN IN DOUBT, FLOG SALES

IN PHASE 1 MOST COMPANIES HAVE FOCUSED on front-line sales, and as table 3.1 indicates, the goal has been revenue quantity. Much of this focus on quantity was based on the assumption that the company carried a heavy load of fixed costs and that greater sales efforts would bring in more revenue, which, when spread over fixed costs, would lead to improved margins.

For regulated industries such as banks and airlines, deregulation brought new pressures. As they looked at other industries that were not regulated or protected, they saw that the fight for customers and market share was much more intense. Businesses like Xerox and IBM were seen to have aggressive sales organizations that could really push the product. In mature industries with similar products,

	Phase 1	Phase 2	Phase 3	Phase 4
Strategy	Sales			
Goal	Quantity			
Problem	Direct & train sales personnel			
Market Focus	Call on everyone			
Product Focus	Core product			
Solution	Selling skills Job definition		© 1993 ActionSystems Inc., Dallas, Texas	

Table 3.1. Sales and Market Management, Phase 1

much of the battle was being won or lost in the sales, distribution, and marketing side of the business.

Many unregulated businesses have also operated in fairly restricted markets due to federal or state laws, patent or copyright protection, capital requirements, market share dominance, or other barriers to entry. As deregulation, expiration of patents, and the opening of global markets began to change the marketplace, companies began to put new focus on sales effectiveness. Hospitals, banks, airlines, public accounting firms, law firms, telecommunication companies, utilities, and many others who had not been particularly sales focused began to play catch-up in this new game. Many of their so-called "sales staff" were not professional salespeople; they were not out in the market prospecting with the initiative and skill required to increase revenue and gain market share; they were merely order takers, and they lacked understanding of the sales process.

For many industries, the solution for Phase 1 was to train and direct people in their new sales roles. They geared up and provided sales training in lock step, expecting great breakthroughs. Unfortunately, they did not take into account the fact that when a whole industry engages in front-line sales training, all companies compete more effectively and dramatic improvements are hard to come by.

A number of companies were disappointed that they did not gain market share, and some discovered that failure to focus on sales could quickly cause a company to lose ground.

The key assumptions behind the Phase 1 solution were these:

■ More revenue will solve about any problem — "Flog 'em again, flog 'em again, harder, harder!"

■ All revenue dollars have the same value and the same cost of sales.

■ Tell them to get out of their office and sell, and good things will happen.

■ Give them professional selling skills and everyone will excel.

Sales training was thought to be like a smallpox vaccination: one dose and you were good for life. Sure enough, the focus on sales roles and training created sales activity and some improved results. Having "solved" the sales problem, executives with short attention spans began asking, "What's next?" But the spike on the sales revenue chart did not last. The momentum created by the training dissipated quickly when people went back into an environment where the risky new selling behaviors were not reinforced. And many salespeople worked in a service role as well — so the more they sold, the more they had to service, and the less time they had to sell.

The consulting and public accounting field provides a good example. In the early 1980s our company was asked to develop a custom sales training program for Arthur Young's (now Ernst & Young) Information Technology Consulting Practice. As one of the "Big Eight" public accounting and consulting firms, they were restricted in direct sales and solicitation by the American Institute of Certified Public Accountants (AICPA). Dick Welsh, national director of information technology at Arthur Young at that time, had been very progressive in hiring "sales" people and initiating the sales focus. His description is apt:

> Every step we took — like the sales training — moved us forward. Yet each step was countercultural because it moved us into a set of skills, practices, and attitudes that were foreign for

the existing culture. It is like a war — take ground and then defend it. If you take more than you can defend, then you give some of it back. The goal is to keep moving forward in a sustainable way.[3]

Moving to a market-driven sales culture was nothing short of pioneering; each step created new breakthroughs — and new obstacles. Astute managers began to lament that they had spent all of this time and money training their salespeople and it was not working. (Actually, it *was* working, but Phase 1 could carry us only so far.) They looked at highly admired sales organizations outside their industry, and quickly saw the importance of sales management in moving to the next level.

PHASE 2: UPGRADING THE QUALITY OF THE FLOGGER

LOOKING AT OTHER INDUSTRIES, management observed that in progressive sales organizations sales managers played a pivotal role (table 3.2). They also saw that these sales managers had grown up in an environment where they had performed as a salesperson under a sales manager. By the time they were promoted to sales manager, the sales management role, practices, and skills had been modeled for them; a system of goal setting, coaching, tracking, and incentives was in place; and their bosses (second-line managers) could mentor them because they had spent time in the sales manager role.

In a sales management training program our firm developed for Frito-Lay, we analyzed the critical behaviors of highly successful sales and sales management personnel. A Frito-Lay executive made this observation:

> We have hired several salespeople from Procter and Gamble. I can ride with a salesperson and in one call I can tell you if he came out of P&G because they have a consistent approach to identifying the needs of the grocery chains — it is very effective. I'll know our managers are good *sales managers* when we have established a reputation with our clients for a consistent, effective, branded approach to uncovering their needs.

	Phase 1	Phase 2	Phase 3	Phase 4
Strategy	Sales	Sales management		
Goal	Quantity	Sustain quantity		
Problem	Direct & train sales personnel	Direct & train managers		
Market Focus	Call on everyone	Call on everyone		
Product Focus	Core product	Core product		
Solution	Selling skills Job definition	Selling skills Job definition		
		Coaching skills Reinforcement Sales tracking	*© 1993 ActionSystems Inc., Dallas, Texas*	

Table 3.2. Sales and Market Management, Phase 2

As the blue-chip sales cultures established a "brand identity" with their clients, other companies began to make strong sales management disciplines and practices a priority. Companies stepped forward to place their wagers in the next race; you could almost read their expressions: "Yeah . . . sales management . . . that's the ticket!"

The goal was to sustain the quantity (revenue) targeted in Phase 1 — the volume increases that management assumed would lead to better profit margins. Management knew that the competition was stiffening, that in many cases deregulation was accelerating, and that without strong sales management the investment made in sales training would be lost. No problem in Phase 2 was more critical than the absence of daily and weekly sales management processes and routines to ensure proactive selling.

Sales management training focused heavily on the setting and tracking of goals, coaching skills, reinforcement, and the use of sales meetings and incentives. The assumptions associated with this focus were these:

- Strong sales managers can add value through goal setting, coaching, and tracking.
- Executives know how to select, evaluate, and coach the coaches (sales managers).
- The critical sales processes, skills, and activities are right as identified — they just need to be managed more effectively.
- Sales managers' salaries can be more than covered by the expected 15 to 25 percent improvement in sales performance of their people.

Introducing strong sales management into a regulated or insulated industry is not child's play. It is more like an organ transplant — the rejection factor is fairly high. Companies that were really committed to it and whose executives stayed focused on it did well. Others, although falling short of their goals, made significant strides. Some, however, were relieved when the sales management wave was over, and retreated to the familiar ground of managing administration, bottom-line numbers, and other things they were comfortable with. Too few mastered the critical skills and activities that lead to strong sales management. The failure to attend to the critical leading indicators such as call activity, sales competencies, coaching, lost business, and bluebirds (sales that come out of the blue), along with longer sales cycles and the rapid advancement and turnover of salespeople, made it difficult to know who was causing what. Sales might go up or down regardless of the sales managers' capabilities.

PHASE 3: GETTING SERIOUS, REMOVING OBSTACLES

MANY COMPANIES BEGAN TO FOCUS on the C-word: *culture* (table 3.3). Management realized that creating a strong sales organization required more than just touching the front-line sales and sales management organizations — it called for a change in all levels and functions of the business. The need for the change was probably most evident in the obstacles that sales managers encountered. As deregulation progressed, mergers quickened, and global and local competition heated up, it became more and more apparent that a real dog fight was coming and, in many cases, industry consolidation was inevitable.

If the game were going to be won or lost based on market share and volume, establishing a strong sales culture was crucial for playing both offense (taking share away) and defense (defending share).

As the game intensified, obstacles began to appear. Sales managers were becoming more and more vocal about what they needed — top management support, better customer information, more effective sales incentive plans, customer-focused products. To create a sales culture, they needed the alignment and support of organization and systems. They could not do it alone.

	Phase 1	Phase 2	Phase 3	Phase 4
Strategy	Sales	Sales management	Sales culture	
Goal	Quantity	Sustain quantity	Increase quantity	
Problem	Direct & train sales personnel	Direct & train managers	Remove obstacles	
Market Focus	Call on everyone	Call on everyone	Everyone call	
Product Focus	Core product	Core product	Multiple products	
Solution	Selling skills Job definition	Selling skills Job definition	Selling skills Job definition	
		Coaching skills Reinforcement Sales tracking	Coaching skills Reinforcement Sales tracking	
			Organization Systems	

© 1993 ActionSystems Inc., Dallas, Texas

Table 3.3. Sales and Market Management, Phase 3

One of the reasons to have "everyone call" was to let staff people experience the challenge of sales and thus be more empathetic to the changes needed for a true sales culture. Sales managers were getting more pressure, but not always more support, because many parts of the company were still in a rejection mode toward this new organ called sales culture.

In Phase 3 many businesses began to focus on multiple products as a way to improve sales efficiency. Some companies tied portions of their incentive programs to cross sales — making multiple sales into a customer account. The problem was that this emphasis sometimes led to the sale of the wrong products, or to the fracturing of sales (rather than one $20,000 sale, how about four $5,000 sales?). Servicing and processing costs went up.

Progressive sales organizations like IBM and Xerox had been innovators and trailblazers in getting to Phase 3. Yet their model, which had brought them success, was being matched by competitors — and it provided no breakthroughs for getting to the next level. In fact, some competitors had developed better distribution systems. For example, Dell Computer used mail-order distribution as a lower-cost, more efficient approach to selling personal computers. Compaq and IBM scrambled to respond.

In implementing Phase 3, managers assumed that —

- Removal of other organizational obstacles would give them the revenue they needed.
- The breakthrough would come from the sales-and-service management practices now in place, once the obstacles were removed.
- Their approach to the marketplace was fine — they just weren't executing it.
- The issue was not cost or efficiency or value — it was a "revenue" problem.
- All that guff from the field about "My market is different" was just resistance to the consistent sales culture they sought.

Playing a Volume Game

Phases 1, 2, and 3 had several things in common. First, the emphasis was on volume — more sales. In a volume game, all sales dollars are equally valuable; they all add to revenue, and the success of a volume focus is measured by product sales. As long as product revenue goals were reached, it was assumed that the sales culture was emerging and that the distribution system was causing it. Second, since sales were reported primarily by product families, it was not possible, or even considered necessary, to track retention and penetration of customer relationships. Third, the primary means for getting the additional sales was by working harder. In essence, management said, "We want more sales efforts, more customers, more product volume — and we want you to get it with less," because most companies were beginning to see the need to hold the line on cost. So with each phase the goals went up, but not the resources. And as Phase 3 came into play, the stereotype of the salesperson on easy street had lost much of its meaning. The old "3–3–3" rule — make three calls, write three orders, and be on the golf course by 3:00 — was history.

The McDonald's Model: Standard and Consistent

Because of the many acquisitions during this period, the merging of different companies, their systems, and their cultures put a premium on consistency and standardization. McDonald's was often used as the model — same products, same service, same signs everywhere. Companies standardized everything possible (hours, products, pricing, facilities, campaigns) to become "one" organization. Many of the mergers were done to buy market share and to reduce costs through economies of scale; staffing models were developed to standardize these cost and staff reductions across a large system. More progressive managers tied their staffing models to numbers of customers or numbers of accounts. Very few tied staffing to profits or market potential. When downsizing came, "share the pain" seemed the fair, consistent way to make it happen.

The Sales Culture Paradigm

Phases 1, 2, and 3 represented a paradigm — a common set of beliefs — about the key elements of a sales culture. At the extreme, this paradigm said that the priorities for a sales and distribution system are these:

- Get product sales regardless of whether you can retain and grow the customers.
- Get volume regardless of whether it is profitable or what the cost of sales or service may be.
- Work harder, no matter how inefficient our approaches (standard campaigns, promotions) — we want it consistent.
- One size fits all, regardless of what customers or local markets may demand.
- Centralized solutions are best because local autonomy will lead to dumb decisions and we'll lose our shirts.
- Across-the-board cost reduction — sharing the pain — will be the fairest approach.

The core belief was that robotic consistency on the sales and distribution side would turn out customers the way Henry Ford's assembly line turned out cars and McDonald's kitchens turned out Big Macs. If your company had a differentiated product or service that was in demand (the only one in town), this approach worked well. However, in a number of instances where differentiation was low, it did not work as intended.

As they focused on selling harder and working harder, most businesses awaited the results and the breakthrough. Company after company tried to flog more customers into the sales pipeline — but no one was guarding the other end. For every 12 accounts opened in retail banking, for example, the industry was closing 10 or 11. The sheer magnitude of "churn and burn" stood squarely in the way of cost control, productivity, and ultimately revenue targets. Improved margins and profits — the milk and honey of the promised land — did not flow according to expectations. Once again, management wandered in search of a better answer.

PHASE 4: A NEW MODEL FOR SALES PRODUCTIVITY

DISCERNING MANAGEMENT BEGAN TO ANALYZE the mission of sales and service. The conventional wisdom had said that volume would lead to profit. However, when it cost too much to acquire new customers, when they did not stay customers, or when they demanded things the company could not supply, volume led not to profit but to cost (table 3.4).

Astute companies began to question the productivity of their sales-and-service organizations. How much of our revenue is a result of our sales distribution system? Can our system acquire and retain customers more efficiently than competitor X? Are we attracting high-profit or just high-cost customers? Does our *sales* process

	Phase 1	**Phase 2**	**Phase 3**	**Phase 4**
Strategy	Sales	Sales management	Sales culture	Market management
Goal	Quantity	Sustain quantity	Increase quantity	Profit
Problem	Direct & train sales personnel	Direct & train managers	Remove obstacles	Costs of sales and service
Market Focus	Call on everyone	Call on everyone	Everyone call	Targeted relationships
Product Focus	Core product	Core product	Multiple products	Multiple products Fee services Relationship value
Solution	Selling skills Job definition	Selling skills Job definition	Selling skills Job definition	Market-segmented sales-&-service skills
		Coaching skills Reinforcement Sales tracking	Coaching skills Reinforcement Sales tracking	Local market analysis & plan
			Organization Systems	Sales, service, & market management

©1993 ActionSystems Inc., Dallas, Texas

Table 3.4. Sales and Market Management, Phase 4

bring value to our customers' *buying* processes, or do they view it as a hassle? If they could buy our products or services at a lower price without a salesperson, would they?

These questions led to better answers. Research on business-to-business selling established that a "fully loaded" sales call could cost $400 to $600, and more if extensive air travel were involved. Financial services businesses calculated that it cost $50 to $75 to open, maintain, and close out certain retail accounts within the first year. People began to say, Wow, acquiring new customers can be very expensive. So if the objective was profit, one of the key problems was cost, specifically cost of sales. An effective sales-and-service system had to be highly productive to overcome such costs.

Not All Customers Are Equal

As management grew more sophisticated about costs, another fact became crystal clear: when it comes to profit contribution, not all customers are equal. In industry after industry — airlines, hotels, retailing, consulting, and banking, to name a few — the Pareto Principle applies: 20 percent of the customers really do contribute 80 percent of the profits.

One of our company's clients, analyzing profit contribution across several hundred bank branches, found 3 percent of their deposit customers contributing over 40 percent of their deposits and 70 percent of their profits. Other clients using profit models are seeing similar concentrations of contribution, often with 10 to 15 percent of the retail and small business customers contributing 90 percent of the profits.

Who Gets What Service?

Another client, one of the largest retail branch systems in North America, discovered that one retail customer contributed more than 20 percent of the profitability in one of its branches. They estimated that it would take 1,400 average customers to replace that one customer, and they had neither the facility nor the staff to handle that many customers. And — you guessed it — no one knew that most valuable customer. Why? Three reasons: no complaints, no visits to the branch, no credit problems. For most branches, the allocation of sales and service time and attention is contingent on loans, complaints, and visits.

This is the case in many service-oriented businesses. We are dispensing sales and service resources mostly to those who come in, complain, and create problems. In essence, the one who demands the most is the one who gets the largest amount of our most valuable resource — the time and expertise of our people. How strange it would be for a product business to sell its different product lines based on the same criteria! Can you imagine going into a car dealership with the money to buy their top-of-the-line Cadillac and the salesperson saying, "Sorry, but we sell Cadillacs only to customers who visit frequently, give us grief, and write hot checks"? How absurd! Yet many service businesses give their top-of-the-line "Cadillac" service to their most demanding customers, while their best and most profitable customers get "Chevy" service. We know how to segment products, but we are much less discerning in delivering segmented sales and service.

When allocating sales and service, we must reflect not only customer needs but their willingness to pay and potential profit contribution. Failure to do so puts us at risk for revenue runoff. Several of our company's banking clients have discovered that 1 to 2 percent of lost customers account for more than 50 percent of their lost deposits. When this loss is analyzed branch by branch, it usually shows that deposit runoff could be cut 50 percent by retaining one customer per branch per month — if it were the right customer. In the September–October 1990 issue of *Harvard Business Review*, Frederick Reichheld of Bain and Company and W. Earl Sasser of the Harvard Business School cite a credit card business's finding that a 2 percent improvement in customer retention is tantamount to a 10 percent reduction in operating cost.[4] We would speculate that retaining the "right" customers equates to significantly more than a 10 percent reduction in operating cost.

FOCUSING ON THE RIGHT CUSTOMERS

SO WHAT DOES IT ALL MEAN? It means that targeting relationships based on their potential contribution is crucial. We cannot push products hard enough, sell hard enough, or work hard enough to overcome focusing on the wrong customers. It also means that acquiring customers will *always* cost too much if we cannot keep them. Part of that retention responsibility belongs to the sales organization to target prospects that are likely to be retainable.

Highly productive sales organizations target customers and prospects for whom multiple product/service sales and line extensions are likely, from whom each repeat sale brings further returns on the initial acquisition cost. And because customers will eventually have the option of buying goods and services without salespeople, the salesperson must deliver value to the buying process. The price the customer is willing to pay for simply filling orders is diminishing; however, helping customers explore unmet needs — educating them — adds value to their buying decisions.

Changing the Paradigm

Discerning companies will concentrate on adding value where customers are willing to pay for it, and lowering costs where they are not. To do this, we must analyze our local markets, target and segment our sales/service efforts, and manage and allocate sales/service resources differently (table 3.5). The new paradigm establishes a new standard and a new level of discipline for sales and service. To parody the old bumper sticker: "Products don't make money, customers do." In our product volume focus, we have acted as though there were an endless line of prospective customers available to us, and an infinite supply of resources to drive them all into the pipeline. But the line of prospects is limited, as are the resources. Our products may be disposable, but our customers are not. To be productive, sales-and-service delivery must retain and cultivate customers in whom substantial sales time and resources have been

Sales Culture Paradigm	Market Management Paradigm
Product push	Customer focus
Volume driven	Profit driven
Work harder	Work smarter
One size fits all (service)	One size fits some
Centralized solutions	Local solutions
Across-the-board cost reduction	Cost reduction against target markets — change service delivery

© 1993 ActionSystems Inc., Dallas, Texas

Table 3.5. Shift to Market Management Paradigm

invested. This means matching sales-and-service strategy to the different needs of markets and their customers.

Sales organizations must produce volume, but those that are highly effective will specialize in *profitable* volume. As a long-term strategy, losing money on customers but making it up on volume is a recipe for disaster. Nor is flogging the troops harder to gain more sales throughput a solution. We will get more energy and commitment only when we define the game so it can be won.

These are the assumptions for Phase 4:

- Revenue does not always equate to profit.

- Some customers are much more profitable than others.

- Profit potential is different in each market, as are customer needs.

- There is not an endless line of prospective customers.

- It is very inefficient to acquire customers who cannot be retained and cultivated.

- Market analysis and planning are required to know whom to target.

- Sales-and-service delivery must be reengineered and resources reallocated in order to be competitive.

Why has the evolutionary path from sales through sales management and sales culture been so difficult? Why has it been so difficult to install effective sales management? Why have we struggled so in creating a sales culture? Is the problem nothing more than the rigors of effecting cultural change?

One of the greatest obstacles is the absence of information, focus, and insight that come out of local market management. How can sales efforts be effective when we are not clear on what types of customers we want, what types of customers are available in the trade area, and how we should allocate our time to them?

How can we make sales management effective when we have no assessment of the local market potential? When we have not set goals on the market mix we are seeking? When we have not identified the critical skills, activities, and resources required to get that mix? When profitable revenue and unprofitable revenue all look the same? When unprofitable customers and activities consume a significant portion of our sales time?

How can we create a sales culture when we lack a process for analyzing the potential and unique needs of local markets in order to optimize what is available? When we are trying to get everyone to "do it the same way," even if that ensures it's wrong in more than half of our local markets? When there is a higher value for compliance than for success? Too often it is not a sales culture we seek, but a culture of standardization and compliance driven by the head office. That is not a sales culture, and it is not customer driven.

PUTTING FIRST THINGS FIRST

IF WE TRULY WANT SALES, sales management, and a sales culture, then we must start with some fundamental answers about market potential, targeted customers, optimal customer mix, and allocation of time and effort. We have had the cart before the horse; Phase 4, Market Management, must become the first step. Analysis, targeting, planning — these are good steps to have *before* implementation.

"Ready, aim, fire!" turns out to be more efficient and more effective than "Fire! Fire! Fire!" With the employees, with the customer, and with the shareholder, we have only so many bullets.

We have gone about as far as we can go with the current model for sales effectiveness. There is no single strategy to fit all target markets, and it can't be micromanaged from the head office. Why? Because doing what works in the local market, within bounds, will be more productive than forcing the same strategy down everyone's throat. We must now change the model and shift gears if we wish to travel at a higher speed with greater efficiency.

4

The Service Quality Wave

Stand Up if the Problem Is Service

66 The purpose of business is
to provide a quality of product
or service that is so good that
the market will be willing to pay
you more than it cost you.
That is an earned profit. 99 [1]

> — *Stanley Marcus*
> *Chairman Emeritus, Neiman Marcus*

*T*HE GAME HAS CHANGED! Throughout the '80s our credo was "More is better" — more luxury, more image, more designer labels, and more service. The prevailing wisdom was, the more service, the better — the customer was willing to pay the difference. Nordstrom was held up as the icon of service quality. Thousands of businesses, hyped on stories of legendary service, ran like lemmings in an attempt to become "the Nordstrom of service," and CEOs dreamed of adorning the cover of *Fortune* or *Forbes* for winning the Malcolm Baldrige National Quality Award. The assumption was that you could never be too thin, too rich, or provide too much service quality.

The '90s brought new insights. The 1990 Malcolm Baldrige winner, Wallace Co., Inc., went into bankruptcy. Federal Express, another Baldrige winner and considered one of the top quality companies in North America, suffered tough times. The Cadillac Division of General Motors won the Baldrige Award but continued to lose market share, even among buyers of American luxury cars.[2]

As the cost of health care marched skyward, *The Wall Street Journal* reported that "as many as one-third of medical procedures may be unnecessary or of little benefit."[3] Meanwhile, Wal-Mart became America's largest retailer based on one overriding theme — value. And as discounting, price cutting, streamlining, and downsizing occurred, one message became very clear: cost matters!

These events do not mean that service quality is passé. In fact, it is probably more important to business success than ever before. But just having a service quality strategy does not guarantee success. Companies will go out of business in large numbers because their approach to service quality does not fit the marketplace. Just as with sales, there has been a series of phases in the evolution of service quality. It is important to understand each phase and its limitations in order to define what we want, and what we do not want, in a service strategy.

PHASE 1: ZERO DEFECTS/COMPLAINTS

THE INITIAL LOOK AT SERVICE QUALITY was focused on fixing things that were broken (table 4.1). Philip Crosby's work on Total Quality Management in the manufacturing sector caught the attention of service industries and helped focus them on the cost of nonconformance to standard.[4] As companies studied cost control, they could see that errors, defects, and complaints were very expensive. Research studies indicated that 25 to 35 percent of operating costs were the result of quality problems.

In the service quality training sessions conducted by ActionSystems, managers often estimated that 20 to 30 percent of their time was spent dealing with quality and customer service problems that were "not done right the first time" or in customer recovery efforts. If the average manager costs $60,000 per year with benefits, that means his or her time alone dealing with conformance could run over $12,000. Across a 2,000-store or -branch system, that means $24 million of first-line manager time, not to mention staff time. Service recovery often means waiving fees, replacing defective

	Phase 1	Phase 2	Phase 3	Phase 4
Strategy	Zero defects/ complaints			
Objective	Cost reduction			
Customer Focus	Retention (defensive & efficient)			
Solution	Standards, control, & centralization			
Leverage	Measurement		*© 1993 ActionSystems Inc., Dallas, Texas*	

Table 4.1. Service Culture Evolution, Phase 1

products, or other forms of customer compensation. As the tip of the iceberg became more visible, companies began to focus on cost reduction as a legitimate objective of service quality.

In addition, the impact of service quality on customer retention became better understood. Research reported by the Technical Assistance Research Program Institute, Inc. (TARP), indicated that 90 percent of customers who are dissatisfied with the service they receive will not buy again or come back.[5] Further, each unhappy customer will, on average, tell his or her story to at least nine people.

Mistakes Cost Money

So, based on this new information, businesses concentrated on service quality as a means for lowering cost and improving retention. The credo essentially became, "Don't screw it up, so you don't run them (customers) off." Borrowed from the methodology of TQM, the solution was to define service quality standards and implement them consistently across the company. These standards included such things as answering the phone by the third ring, not letting customer wait time exceed a certain number of minutes, and allowing no more than "x" errors per 1,000 customer statements. Conformance to standards would be measured, and nonconformance would not be tolerated.

The assumptions for Phase 1 were these:

- All customers want the same things — the basics.
- Fewer defects equals less cost
- Fix things customers complain about, have problems with, or whatever is broken.
- Customers will then be happy and will stay.
- Retention will enhance profits.

By and large, the assumptions were not wrong; unfortunately, they did not represent the whole truth. It was a good start; it got everyone going and fixed some problems that needed fixing. But it was the first quarter of the first game — not an end-of-the-season Super Bowl victory.

PHASE 2: PROMISES OF GREAT SERVICE

AS THE MOVIE PROMO LOUDLY WHISPERS, "Just when you thought it was safe to go back in the water," we began to hear of breakthrough, legendary service — service so good that not only did it reduce cost and enhance retention, it caused everyone to want to be your customer (table 4.2). The book *Service America* by Karl Albrecht and Ron Zemke described the terrific turnaround by the Scandinavian Airlines System (SAS) based on a fanatical commitment to service by its leader Jan Carlzon.[6] Carlzon's book *Moments of Truth* later chronicled the story and captured the spirit of inspired leadership focused on service quality.[7] Other books, such as *In Search of Excellence*, reinforced the opportunities for success through quality.[8]

In Phase 2, Nordstrom's department store became recognized as the Pied Piper of service. The lesson of Phase 2 was that the absence of defects is not the same as the presence of value. An Edsel repaired is still an Edsel. What was needed was Mercedes service for everyone. The assumption was that no matter how much service you provided, it would pay off in retention, repeat business, referrals, and word of mouth. The goal was undifferentiated revenue growth. You didn't want just segments of the market — you wanted all of it.

	Phase 1	Phase 2	Phase 3	Phase 4
Strategy	Zero defects/ complaints	Great service		
Objective	Cost reduction	Undifferentiated revenue growth		
Customer Focus	Retention (defensive & efficient)	Attraction (offensive & volume)		
Solution	Standards, control, & centralization	Inspire & empower		
Leverage	Measurement	Leadership & communication		© 1993 ActionSystems Inc., Dallas, Texas

Table 4.2. Service Culture Evolution, Phase 2

And although astute observers knew that Nordstrom's upscale customer base was narrow and finite and that not everyone was willing to pay for legendary service, people got carried away. The wave engulfed them. In fact, a good way to get thrown out was to question any part of the great-service strategy.

Going on Offense

Obtaining market share was seen as a highly successful profit strategy as carried out by the Japanese. Numerous studies showed that the companies that had dominant industry market share tended to be the most profitable. Jack Welch, CEO at General Electric and one of the most respected executives in the U.S., said they would not stay in any business in which they could not be number one or two.[9]

With market share as the goal, great service was designed to keep current customers and, more importantly, to attract a lot of new ones. Service would become a way to go on the offensive.

If Phase 1 was based on designing very specific rules and standards, Phase 2 was characterized by the philosophy behind Stew Leonard's dairy, which was immortalized by Tom Peters.[10] Stew had two rules —

Rule 1: The customer is always right.

Rule 2: If the customer is ever wrong, see Rule 1.

Phase 2 said, in effect, The heck with lots of rules and procedures, it all comes down to one thing: delight the customer. Jan Carlzon, Tom Peters, and many others preached the E-word: empowerment. Create a vision, inspire and enlist your people, and then empower them to achieve it. Use leadership and communication to make it happen. Phase 2 provided a powerful, positive, and humanistic message: Do whatever it takes. Don't use company policy or standards as a reason not to take care of the customer. You are the customer's advocate. Exceed their expectations every time.

It was optimistic and uplifting — and a little confusing, particularly for people working in banks, airlines, food service, and other industries where people's lives, health, and money were on the line. The security, control, and trust issues associated with being the custodian of the customer's well-being made it unclear when to follow the rules and when to break the rules. Breaking the rules was not the same as being customer driven if a customer wound up being defrauded or ripped off or hurt. On the other hand, following the rules sometimes seemed merely irritating and unresponsive to customers.

The assumptions for Phase 2 were the following:

- We make money on all customers.
- We can never provide too much customer service.
- We should get as many customers as possible.
- The cost of acquiring and retaining customers will always be exceeded by their revenue.
- If we inspire and empower our people with the vision, we will be pleased with their application and its results.
- Providing the best possible service to everyone is morally the right thing to do.

As did Phase 1, great service solved some of the problems. It was particularly useful in dealing with bureaucratic rules, rigid procedures, and unresponsive ways of handling customers. It represented progress. But it was not the destination of the journey — only an intermediate stop. The assumptions were generally correct, but carried to their extreme, they created more problems. And although the passion and dogma were so strong in many companies that it was risky to question the strategy, if you listened closely you could hear whispers: "Yeah, but some customers take more service than they pay for" or "Why spend more money on customers who already cost too much?" or "Boy, this is getting expensive," or "What if a lower price is what they really want?"

PHASE 3: PRODUCT AND SERVICE SEGMENTATION

ONCE AGAIN THE ISSUES RAISED by the current service quality phase led to the next phase (table 4.3). Businesses began to develop more effective models to assess customer profitability. It quickly became apparent that certain customer groups were much more profitable than others. As we have seen before, the information was startling — in many businesses 10 to 15 percent of the customers contributed 80 to 90 percent of the profits. The 20–80 rule actually understated the case.

Marketing departments began to calculate the value of increasing their share of these highly profitable market segments. Airlines introduced frequent-flier programs to reward highly profitable business travelers for loyalty. Hotels and car rental companies followed suit.

When research indicated that the seniors market was a lucrative segment because of high deposit balances, retail banks implemented micromarketing: direct mail campaigns, targeted advertisements, and development of special products such as seniors programs. The objective of this centrally deployed strategy was to increase revenue growth in the high-profit market segments by creating specialized

	Phase 1	Phase 2	Phase 3	Phase 4
Strategy	Zero defects/ complaints	Great service	Product segmentation	
Objective	Cost reduction	Undifferentiated revenue growth	Revenue growth — high-profit market segments	
Customer Focus	Retention (defensive & efficient)	Attraction (offensive & volume)	Segmentation (focused)	
Solution	Standards, control, & centralization	Inspire & empower	Segmented products	
Leverage	Measurement	Leadership & communication	Marketing programs	

© 1993 ActionSystems Inc., Dallas, Texas

Table 4.3. Service Culture Evolution, Phase 3

products with features attractive to the target market. These features, heavily promoted in marketing campaigns, would cause the target market to self-select and come to us. In essence, the marketing would drive target customers into the stores or branches. This approach contrasted strongly with Phase 2, which went after everyone with little thought given to specific groups.

Looking for Mr. Right

This new focus was clearly a breakthrough, an opportunity to be more effective in sales and service; by targeting specific groups, we could deliver more effectively to their unique needs. Most organizations, however, faced challenges. For one thing, the targeting of customer segments was not at first fully thought out. For example, seniors were a good target group on which to focus in banking; from a micromarketing standpoint it was an easy group to identify and reach. The problem was that although one portion of the seniors market (the high-deposit seniors) contributed large profits, other portions provided very low deposits but were very expensive and time consuming to service. The centralized marketing campaigns tended to attract loss leaders to local branches that had high concentrations of these low-deposit/high-service seniors in their trade areas.

Centralized marketing did not get enough involvement and input from the store or branch system, nor was it always attentive to the diverse trade areas served by local units. In essence, the local units were operating in Phase 1 (zero defects) or Phase 2 (great service), while the head office was micromarketing in Phase 3.

The customers who were attracted to the stores and branches often encountered a staff and system that were not prepared to deliver the promises implied in the ads. Since marketing campaigns tend to attract customers and prospects who are easily influenced by all marketing messages, this group tended to be more transient than we might have wished, and we did not get as many of them to "stick" as we should have. It also created frustration for the staff. As one customer service representative described it:

We are busting a gut trying to provide great service to everyone, and now we keep getting pounded by marketing to support the micromarketing efforts. We have all these seniors
coming in who require lengthy explanations of how the seniors
program works, and we just don't have time to get it all done.
In fact, no one has been trained to explain the program. The
advertising had already started when we got the brochures. Of
course, the customers complained when no one knew anything
about their "program." Unfortunately, most of the seniors coming into our branch have very small deposits and they need
help balancing their checkbooks.

Thus, the strategy and focus for Phase 3 were very positive, but
execution often lacked planning and alignment with local branches
and stores to take into account their diverse trade areas.

The key assumptions for Phase 3 were these:

- Some customer groups are much more profitable than others.

- We can design product and service features that will attract
  these groups.

- We can use central micromarketing to identify them, target
  them, and communicate with them about our products and
  services.

- When they come to the store or branch, they will get what
  they expected and will become loyal, profitable customers.

- This change in the mix of profitable customers will increase
  local profits.

Although poor implementation and execution diluted the
potential, these assumptions represented real progress and opportunity, which paved the way for Phase 4.

PHASE 4: CUSTOMER VALUE

AS PEOPLE LOOKED BACK AT PHASES 1, 2, AND 3, they saw a lot of
good ideas: fewer defects, less cost, better retention, great service,
service as an offensive weapon, measurement, empowerment, focus

	Phase 1	Phase 2	Phase 3	Phase 4
Strategy	Zero defects/ complaints	Great service	Product segmentation	Customer value
Objective	Cost reduction	Undifferentiated revenue growth	Revenue growth — high-profit market segments	Right sales & service at the right cost
Customer Focus	Retention (defensive & efficient)	Attraction (offensive & volume)	Segmentation (focused)	Profitability through retention & attraction of right customers
Solution	Standards, control, & centralization	Inspire & empower	Segmented products	Market-driven sales, service, costs
Leverage	Measurement	Leadership & communication	Marketing programs	Local market management

©1993 ActionSystems Inc., Dallas, Texas

Table 4.4. Service Culture Evolution, Phase 4

on high-profit customer groups, and micromarketing (table 4.4). The problem was that they were treating the ideas in different ways, the way the fabled 11 blind men from Pakistan perceived the elephant in 11 different ways. None of them were wrong, but none of their perceptions constituted the whole truth, nor were their ideas knitted together to constitute a winning service strategy or a winning set of practices.

As we moved into the decade of the '90s, some of these practices represented out-and-out contradictions for many businesses. We were still mouthing the service mantras of the '80s — great service, zero defects — while we continued to deal with the reality of becoming a lower-cost producer. The inconsistencies of these messages were obvious to our front-line people. As one customer representative described it in a recent training session:

> The executives keep standing up in front of us and preaching the importance of customer service, yet we keep reducing the number of staff in our branch. I'll know they are serious about service when they hire some more people — so we can shorten the lines. Until then, it's kind of hard for me to get real excited about customer service. In fact, the whole thing makes me a little cynical.

Even Tom Peters, the excellence guru, addressing a group in Toronto, said, "We blew it with our first three books."[11] He emphasized that the customer was still king but that in many companies we couldn't get close to the customer because of the bureaucracy and cost.

Many service training programs kept pushing Phase 2 service — the more the better — while top management was trying to cut costs. In the eyes of the service delivery staff, the two did not fit. The ads told customers to expect Cadillac service, even as we were cutting the number of service staff. We were writing hot checks, making promises we could not keep. Executives were looking for a free lunch — better service with less cost, but without a game plan to bridge the gap. It is no wonder that customers were disappointed, executives lost credibility, and workers became more tired, stressed, and cynical.

Innovative competitors took advantage of the chaos. Discounters presented customers an option: Since you are not getting valued service anyway, we will bring you a lower price.

VALUE: WHAT THE CUSTOMER IS WILLING TO PAY FOR

SO, WHICH IS IT? "TASTES GREAT!" OR "LESS FILLING!"? To reconcile "great service" vs. "less cost," we must come face to face with the concept of value.

Service quality is a wonderful thing. Customers will take as much as we give them for free. The acid test for value, however, is not, Can we give it away? but rather, Are we providing something customers are willing to pay us a profit to produce and deliver? For our sales-and-service delivery system, the question is, Can it deliver value across markets and across large groups of customers?

A recent survey by Deloitte & Touche published in *ADWEEK* drives home the point that in many cases retailers are not in sync with consumers regarding what they value in choosing a store (fig. 4.1). The importance of service appears dramatically lower than retailers expected. This seems to indicate that the value added by

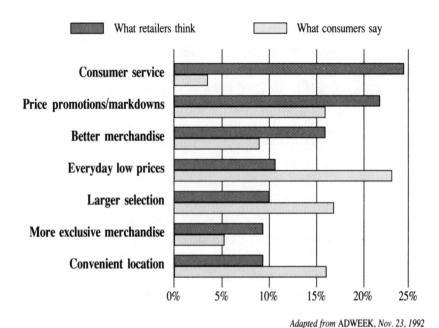

Adapted from ADWEEK, *Nov. 23, 1992*

Figure 4.1. Why Consumers Pick a Store

retail salespeople is low, especially compared with the value of everyday low prices. Larger selection and convenient locations were also more important to customers than retailers thought.

Creating Value

Focusing on value means being more effective in assessing the things we do, could do, or could eliminate in the service delivery chain to create value. A good example of this is the car dealership cited earlier that eliminated its sales force and doubled its sales in a month. The automobile industry has been measuring customer satisfaction and providing customer sales-and-service training for years, yet the Florida dealer "discovered" what we have known all along: the traditional car-buying process is a hassle. Eliminating the hassle creates value. Now a number of dealerships have gone to this concept.

Focusing on value does not mean neglecting such qualities as reliability, responsiveness, and assurance. Rather, it means clients may be more discerning than ever about what they will pay for service. Most people really do think Rolls Royce is the finest car, but few are willing to pay the price to own one. Almost everyone enjoys good service at a gas station, but most would rather pump their own gas than pay for the station attendant's service.

Yes, the basics still matter. The warm smile, friendly service, and helpful recommendations all still matter. Yes, preventing defects and service problems is usually less expensive than fixing them. But management must always decide which defects to correct first and which service delivery enhancements — that add value — will be its priority to install. Customers have more choices than ever of prices and service levels available, and will base their choices on perceived value. Therefore, if value is what they are buying, we must make our business good at creating value — value determined by weighing the importance of service delivery relative to its cost.

The real breakthroughs in value cannot always be acquired by simply working harder; innovation is often necessary. And often that innovation is tied to the unique needs and opportunities of a local market. A dentist with a specialized children's practice in a large shopping mall figured out a way to help moms who were accustomed to waiting while he worked on their children: he gave them beepers, so they could shop until he beeped them to communicate that their child's appointment was finished — a service innovation, targeted to a specific group, that clearly added value.

LOWER COST AND HIGHER REVENUE

PHASE 4 IS DESIGNED TO CREATE CUSTOMER VALUE by providing the right sales and service at the right cost. Balancing these factors with the customer's wants and needs creates a winning customer strategy; trying to create an effective approach to customer management by focusing on just one is like designing a one-legged stool. Done well, however, the right sales and right service at the right cost increases profitability by attracting and keeping the right customers — those who value what we are good at and are willing to pay for it. This is particularly relevant in industries where a significant portion of customers lose us money.

Phase 4 implies that the outcome of effective service quality is both lower cost and higher revenue — because it eliminates things that do not bring value and replaces them with things that do. William H. Davidow, in the July–August 1989 *Harvard Business Review*, outlined the perils of getting it wrong:

> Developing a service (and market segment) strategy is an essential step toward choosing an optimal mix and level of service for different customer sets. Provide too little service, or the wrong kind, and customers will leave; provide too much, even the right kind, and your company will go broke or price itself out of the market.[12]

Thomas H. Davenport, author of *Process Innovation — Reengineering Work through Information Technology*, makes a key point about service and quality — that it must have an aim:

> High-quality, low-cycle-time products and services are only useful if they fit the external environment and satisfy a customer demand. This is not always the case with companies that make quality — which is not a strategy, but a way of implementing strategy — a key aspect of their strategies.[13]

Quality is not a strategy, and neither is service. Wal-Mart took a market by storm — not by increasing service, but by increasing value. Southwest Airlines has become one of the most profitable airlines flying by eliminating meals and reserved seats. And, yes, their quality is very good, but it is the *value* they deliver that makes them so attractive to customers. Nordstrom continues with its legendary service, but it is focused on a target market that values this level of service and is willing to pay for it — in price, repeat business, and loyalty.

The objective of Phase 4 is to make our service quality truly market driven — tested and found true by customers who are willing to pay us a profit. Service and quality become an integral part of our market strategy when we can answer these questions: "Toward what end?" "Who do we wish to attract, grow, and retain?" "What do they value?" Answering these questions would be far easier if all customers and all markets valued exactly the same things. But many of their wants and needs are different, and much of what they value is determined by the hours, location, staff, and skills of the local unit. Phase 4 service quality means adjusting many of these variables locally. It also means identifying the needs that can best be met through lower-cost, more efficient central delivery mechanisms such as 1-800 service and sales.

In today's world, these needs change rapidly. Federal Express is one of the highest-quality companies in the world, yet almost overnight the fax machine took a large bite out of its business. Two decades earlier Xerox spent hundreds of millions of dollars unsuccessfully trying to market fax technology. As needs evolve and trade areas change, being market driven means conducting a never-ending quest to understand what the customer values *now*.

The assumptions of Phase 4 are these:

- Customers are different in their needs, wants, willingness to pay, and potential profit contribution to the company.

- Service delivery should be designed and allocated based on customers' needs, wants, willingness to pay, and potential contributions.

- Differing levels of service are needed to carry this out — one size does not fit all.

- The best-designed service must be tailored to the nuances and potential of the local market.

- The way to optimize value to the customer, the employee, and the shareholder is to deliver the right service to the right customer at the right cost.

Lessons Learned

To summarize, most service cultures go through several phases in refining their initiatives to become market driven. The phases, and the lessons learned from them, are as follows:

Phase 1: Zero Defects/Complaints

The lesson: We must move beyond zero defects because, for the customer, the absence of defects is not the same as the presence of value.

Phase 2: Great Service for Everyone

The lesson: Great service from the customers' point of view is a wonderful thing, but the real test is, Are they willing to pay us a profit to deliver it?

Phase 3: Product Segmentation for Target Groups

The lesson: Product segmentation with special features for high-value, "franchise" customers is a good start, but it does not address the value of human delivery of the product at the local distribution point.

Phase 4: Customer Value

The lesson: Customer value means delivering the right service to the right customers at the right cost.

As we look at the evolution of service culture strategy, we come back to some familiar questions. Why have we been disappointed in both the dedication to the service cause and the results of installing a service culture? Certainly the challenges of cultural change explain part of it.

In my view, the challenge of installing and sustaining a service culture is very similar to our dilemma in the sales culture. How can we efficiently and effectively fix the defects or provide great service if we don't know which customers we are going after or what they want? How can we target products to certain groups with no attention to service delivery for them? We can't.

Service and sales must start with assessing our market, identifying our targets, and designing our sales-and-service delivery accordingly. We cannot progress any further until we stop and change the model. Anything short of changing the approach will limit our productivity and result in a chaotic, confused, and demoralized work force — which makes winning any war impossible.

More specifically, failure to change leads to four critical risks that are capable of putting a company out of business. Those risks are the subject of the next chapter.

5

Peril on the Customer Side

Managing Customer and Market Risks

66 It seems to me you lived your life
like a candle in the wind,
never knowing who to cling to
when the rain set in. 99[1]

> — *"Candle in the Wind"*
> *by Elton John and Bernie Taupin*

*T*HE MANAGEMENT OF RISK IS CRUCIAL in any business. Some industries have particularly high risk exposures that represent a key component of their business. For example, the insurance industry gets paid to insure individuals and organizations against medical, property, and other risks. The attest function of public accounting firms is designed to assure shareholders of public companies that certain generally accepted accounting principles were followed in reporting financial results. Bonding of general contractors in the construction business is used to manage the risks associated with large construction projects. In the investment and brokerage industry, great emphasis and very specific disclaimers are used to explain the risk to the investor. And, certainly in banking, credit risk is of paramount importance in making recoverable loans to individual and business borrowers.

Virtually all industries in which significant business risk has been identified have tracking mechanisms, early warning devices, and other control mechanisms to manage the risk effectively. Yet the sales-and-service distribution systems of many companies experience significant undetected risk — risk that puts the enterprise on the bubble. Silent erosion of share of wallet from its best customers, loss of highly profitable customers and their replacement by more expensive and less profitable customers, and service delivery approaches that are too expensive for certain market segments are just a few of the risks. Sometimes these risks show up as a decline in revenue. Too often, however, revenue may remain stable or even grow, but margins may shrink and sales or servicing costs may rise.

These customer and market risks can go unnoticed and yet be deadly. Most companies have only begun to learn how to forecast, assess, and manage these risks market by market. Traditional measures of product revenue, customer satisfaction, and market share may tell us little about what may be a malignancy in key target groups within our local market.

How did we get here? By participating in a series of waves that treat the symptoms — poor sales, problem service, too much cost — without focusing on the whole. Each solution focused the business on the symptoms of one problem while distracting it from the others. There are predictable risks that come out of this fragmented, symptom-based approach to managing.

This chapter reexamines traditional sales-and-service delivery systems in terms of four critical risks:

- Retention risk
- Growth and penetration risk
- Attraction risk
- Managed cost risk

The financial results and ultimately the viability of any business enterprise are driven by these four factors. In a service-oriented business, they take on even greater importance.

We can look at these risks in terms of individual customers and prospects, or we can apply the same approach to whole markets or target groups within a market. In either case, these risks have historically been underemphasized and undermanaged because the trends are usually hard to detect until they show up as revenue or profit losses. These risks do not make business headlines like Hurricane Andrew for the insurance business, or Ernst & Young's $400 million settlement with the FDIC for alleged lapses in its audit work with banks and thrifts, or Olympia and York's gargantuan credit default on banks around the world.[2] Yet those industries have given extensive attention to managing their risks; some of the risks were insured, some were accrued over several years, and in some cases reserves were set aside in anticipation of the risk. Most companies are much less skilled at deploying their sales-and-service distribution systems to manage customer and market risk. Let's look at these risks individually.

RISK 1: RETENTION

SIMPLY STATED, RETENTION RISK is the risk of losing the business of existing customers. In businesses that have a few large clients, such as advertising, public accounting, and corporate banking, there is usually great emphasis on retention and great distress if defection occurs. However, in consumer-type businesses where there are thousands or millions of customers, this risk has been much less discernible.

Keeping Customers for Life

In the past five years compelling research has emerged that helps us understand the risks and opportunities of customer retention. The TARP studies, which focused on the lifetime value of customers, estimated that the lifetime value of a loyal customer to the automotive industry is more than $150,000 in revenue.[3] A married couple with 2.2 kids is worth more than $264,000 in lifetime revenue to a grocery chain. Frequent fliers who travel over a million miles are worth well over a quarter of a million dollars in revenue to an airline. Certainly, the defection of these types of customers represents significant risk.

Bain and Company, a global consulting firm, found that customer retention has a strong impact on profitability in a number of industries. The analysis focused on assessing the net present value of customers and their impact on profitability if an additional 5 percent were retained (fig. 5.1).

Although some of the specifics have been debated, the general conclusions are solid. One, the cost of customer acquisition is high, so the longer we keep the customer, the more we can spread the cost. Two, the cost to replace a lost customer is high, but failure to do so leaves fixed overhead cost that is not covered.[4] The longer the life of the relationship, the higher the net present value. Although we have always known that losing customers was bad, we have not had a reliable way to quantify the actual financial impact — and as long as revenue was stable or growing, it was easy to overlook the incremental profits lost and the increased cost of sales caused by customer turnover.

The Cost of Silent Erosion

When our company runs training sessions with managers, we are often surprised by the number who say that retention is not a

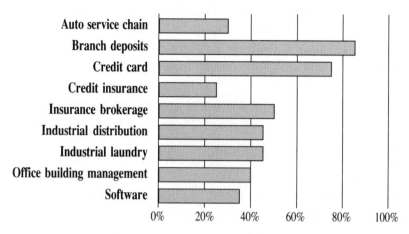

Profit Impact of 5% Retention Rate Increase on Customer Value

Adapted from Loyalty/Retention Practice, ©Bain & Company, Inc.

Figure 5.1. How Does Customer Retention Impact Profitability?

problem, that relatively few customers are leaving. Yet when we distinguish retention of share of wallet — our share of the customer's total business — we find that while we haven't totally lost the customer, we may have lost much of his business to our competitors.

We don't have to look very far to find glaring examples of customer retention problems: IBM, large department stores, American autos, the banking industry. These defections first show up as blips in a few local markets. California markets led the foreign-car defection parade. Regional rural markets are where Wal-Mart began to cut into major retailers such as Sears. Yet if all we are watching is overall revenues and bottom-line profits, the erosion may be barely discernible. In fact, in a growing marketplace and economy, it may be invisible at the aggregate level. Local customer retention is a crucial early warning tool for savvy market-driven companies. Yet most businesses are so addicted to product targets, revenues, and profits that they fail to look closely enough at the local market fundamentals that drive the business.

Insurance companies, accounting firms, and banks will eventually pay off catastrophic losses like Hurricane Andrew, FDIC, and Olympia & York. However, the risk of customer defections in any business, resulting in lifetime decisions by buyers, will cause us to miss revenue and kidnapped profits year after year. Table 5.1 shows a hypothetical example.

For simplicity, let's assume that each customer has an average buying "lifetime" of 10 years, so that the easy calculation (ignoring the time value of money) would show that the local franchise has a group of customers with an income stream worth over $5 million ($500,000 × 10 years) in potential future profits. Five million dollars! As steward of this income stream, the market manager must secure, protect, and expand these future profits over time.

When we get as serious about customer management and market management as we are about other forms of risk management, we will apply a similar level of rigor to forecasting, managing, tracking, and accounting for customer retention — particularly the 10 to 15 percent of the customers who provide 80 to 90 percent of the profits. We will build a fence around these customers, and we will do it locally, market by market.

Existing customers are an asset with a predictable income stream. The potential of losing those dollars is a very real risk. The magnitude of this risk warrants a level of discipline in our management processes to forecast, anticipate, track, and apply early warning mechanisms to manage this exposure. Because of the way we

Revenue:	$5 million
Profit:	$500,000
Customers:	5,000
Customer Profitability:	$100 annual profit per customer

Table 5.1. XYZ Corporation: Local Branch or Store

have historically tracked revenue, customer satisfaction, and profits without focusing on retention risk, the silent erosion of share of wallet and market penetration has been camouflaged. In the '80s we could get by with doing it that way; today it is no longer tolerable, because it can put us out of business. The current margins and competitive pressures do not permit loose customer management. Market managers must become stewards over the income stream of local trade areas. They cannot afford to trade in their most valuable customers for low-profit customers, and they cannot in any event afford customer defection. They must use retention as their primary local strategy to manage defection risk.

RISK 2: GROWTH

GROWTH OR PENETRATION RISKS OCCUR when more than one provider serves a customer. The risk is that someone else will grow our customers. These "split connections" mean that customers are making decisions every day about where their expenditure stream (and your revenue stream) will be directed. Although we often think of our relationship with a customer as a marriage, research is compelling that for many businesses, most customers have many other relationships.

Think of your own buying decisions. How many places do you buy groceries and household items? Perhaps one or two grocery stores, a convenience store, and certain items from a discount store like Sam's Wholesale Club or Price Club. How about financial services? Research shows that the upscale user of financial services is likely to be doing business with four, six, or ten different institutions (considering credit cards, auto loans, mutual funds, retirement accounts, home mortgages, and transaction accounts).[5] In the typical bank, well over 70 percent of the customers have accounts elsewhere, and for each dollar of deposit with that bank, customers will average $1 to $3 elsewhere. Yes, infidelity is rampant! Customers are running around on us, and that can lead to divorce.

The Cost of Customer Infidelity

Why is business so fragmented? The easy answer is that one company cannot meet all the needs of a customer in a category such as groceries, fast food, or financial services. But this is nowhere near the whole truth. Customers' buying patterns directly reflect many companies' selling patterns. In most businesses, what do we promote? We give coupons for grocery items that encourage buyers to shop at several stores for the anointed products. At the end of the day, the grocery industry has served, processed, and checked out two to three times as many customers (assuming each shopper went to two or three stores) for no additional revenue.

When the next special comes along, it starts all over again. Each time it happens, the store takes on underpriced business. Why? Because most industries focus on growing product revenue instead of growing customers. The profitability of these promoted sales is much lower than the regular sales. In retailing, Sears provides an instructive example. By running its business for years on specials, it trained its customers to await the sale. Wal-Mart and Target, by contrast, trained their customers to come in for everyday low prices.

The revenue and cost risk for doing business the old way are real and the exposure is high. How high? Let's look again at our XYZ branch (table 5.1). If we assume 70 percent of our customer base does as much business with other providers as with us, and that business is roughly as profitable as ours, then we are leaving a profit potential of $350,000 ($500,000 × 70 percent) on the table. Those dollars represent missed opportunities. But that is just the beginning of the problem. If the other providers figure out that their customers are doing business with us, then *they* will go after *our* business. In such case, 70 percent of our current profits, or $350,000, is at risk; losing that would leave us with a profit of only $150,000. (In reality it might leave us with less than zero, because a good portion of our fixed cost would be difficult to unload.) That is exactly what our astute competitors understand. As they get market focused and customer driven, they will do what the airlines have done with their frequent-flier programs: they will promote owning and growing customers. Pushing products is tantamount to being in the customer-rental business — a short-term, transient business at best.

Imagine a $10 billion company, making $1 billion a year, having 70 percent of its earnings wiped out by the mass defection of all its "split connections." Consider that this $700 million earnings defection will also be missing next year and the year after, since those customers will be difficult to win back. Consider the massive layoffs and cost reductions that will be required, since the organization is now overstaffed and over-resourced. Would any company intentionally take on this risk? It wouldn't happen overnight, and that's too bad, because if it did, it would get our attention and we could take action to prevent it. But if erosion occurs quietly over two or three years, we seem hardly to notice. This is not a theoretical argument; it has already happened to the banks, whose best customers have quietly slipped away to mutual funds and brokerage firms. It has happened to IBM, to Sears, and to General Motors. It happened to Xerox when its copier market share fell from the high 80s to the chilly 30s.

Managing Customer Infidelity

Growth risk is real — in terms of both missed opportunities and customer defection. This is one reason that cross-sell ratios (the number of products sold per customer), although important, are not nearly as powerful a tool as knowing the business our customers have elsewhere. In fact, a depth or penetration ratio can be a valuable tool to help us estimate the percentage we have of a customer's overall business. If we gather this kind of information as part of a customer profile, it can also be fairly accurate.

The goal is penetration and consolidation of the relationship. If we get all of the customer's business, three things happen:

1. Cross-sell ratios increase dramatically.

2. Defection risk goes down.

3. Forecasts for current and future profitability rise dramatically.

None of this is news. It is common sense, but it is not common practice. We talk about the risk daily, but in many companies we have not put in place a mechanism to fully manage this risk. We are not forecasting, tracking, or managing this risk locally. We are not quantifying the amount of growth potential in our existing customer base or setting goals or tracking progress against those goals. Alarms should go off if we are not gaining penetration of our customer base, streetcorner by streetcorner. We must know locally: if we could upsell (move from a C to a B or an A) only one customer in our unit next year, who would it be? We must know who has the greatest potential for enhancing our franchise. If our sales-and-service distribution system is going to be highly productive, it must continuously improve its performance in the war for penetration and growth of our local target customer groups.

RISK 3: ATTRACTION

ATTRACTION RISK COMES IN TWO VARIETIES. First, there is the risk that the customers we attract will not be profitable. This can happen if the cost of obtaining them is too high. The Council on Financial Competition estimates that a small- to medium-sized business customer ($5 million to $50 million in revenue) costs financial service providers an average of $5,000 to acquire.[6] This makes sense when we consider the number of single business-to-business sales calls (at $400 to $600 each) and joint calls required to bring in each new customer.

In fact, wouldn't it be interesting if a salesperson had to pick up a $500 check before going on each call? Imagine the discussion between the salesperson and the manager:

Salesperson: I've got a call this afternoon on Widget Manufacturing.

Manager: Good — go get 'um.

Salesperson: I need $500.

Manager: Uh huh.

Salesperson: In fact, I really will need more than that, now that I think about it. I mean, I probably won't get their business on the first call — it'll probably take at least five calls . . . so I guess I'll need you to give me a check for $2,500. And I may need some more later.

Manager: Who did you say you're calling on? What kind of potential do you think they represent?

We hear managers say again and again that, as they review call reports, they often wonder about 20 to 30 percent of the calls. They lament that many seem to be low-potential, high-risk long shots or the appointments easiest to get, but not necessarily the ones they need to build their local franchise. But as long as the emphasis is on volume, sales staff will go after the short-term, easy hits, because all sales lead to revenue volume, profitable or not, high cost or not, sustainable or not, in the target market or not. The course of least resistance is not always the best course — but it is the easiest one.

The Cost of Getting the Wrong Customers

In many cases, the cost of the sale alone should be evidence that some business is not worth the acquisition cost or that other targets may give a better return. But when we do not know what our cost of sales is locally, it is quite difficult to allocate and manage sales resources effectively.

Cost of sales is not the only reason that attraction efforts do not pay off. Sometimes the cost of servicing, or the credit risk, or the size of the combined revenues, or pricing, or the tenure, or the monitoring, or any number of other factors may keep the acquisition cost from paying off. There are certain market segments that are inherently more expensive to service or more likely to defect.

We must think of acquisition cost as a scarce resource, like capital, and ask the question, "What prospecting effort will give us the greatest return?" If our unit could make only one prospect call next year, are we clear on what the profile would look like? Do we know specifically who on our prospect list best fits that profile? What if we could make five calls? Twenty-five calls?

Just because we have referrals or easy access to a prospect does not mean he or she should be at the top of the list — even though ease of access is one factor. In fact, walk-ins and untargeted referrals often add randomness to our customer mix and serve to dilute profitability. If we get only those who seek us out, we may not be pleased to discover that we got only what none of our competitors wanted.

Several years ago our consultants were working with a large retail bank to install local market management in one of its downtown branches. As we began the process, the branch manager was describing how good business had been the past few weeks. The lobby was full, the lines were long; business was really good. By the end of the process, in analyzing the kind of customers the branch was attracting, he discovered that a competitor had demarketed its worst customers into his branch. As a result, his costs had gone up, service had gone down, and his attention to his best customers had decreased. We often worry about what happens if we lose our best customers to the competition — but if the competition really wants to hurt us, they will send us their worst customers. How could that happen to us? By striving for product revenue and volume without focusing on who it comes from.

Attracting Profits vs. Attracting Costs

The second risk is that, with all our costs, we are not attracting new customers. A disclaimer here is important. Certainly, in many local markets where market share is high, retention and growth of targeted high-value customers is going to be a much higher priority than attraction of new ones. This is especially true if sheer volume makes it difficult to give them the appropriate attention.

However, according to The Council on Financial Competition, in most banks 10 to 20 percent of the retail and small business customers turn over each year.[7] Sanford Rose, writing for the *American Banker*, said, "A shift in the customer mix from 30 [percent A's]–30 [percent B's]–40 [percent C's] to 40–30–30 — that is, a 10 percentage point increase in the number of A's — can often raise overall retail profits by as much as 60 percent."[8]

If a 10 percent change in the mix can raise our profits 60 percent, what are we doing to create the desired mix in a given trade area? What are we doing to make the franchise more valuable 12 months from now? Conversely, if a competitor takes 10 percent of our best customers, we could experience a 60 percent decline in profits — a harrowing thought.

Clearly, attracting new customers is one way to improve the mix. And to do so with intention and purpose can be very rewarding. But there is a risk that we will attract customers without changing the mix. In working with hundreds of local units to assess their mix, our company has found that a 5 to 10 percent change directed at high-profit target groups can lead to a 20 to 30 percent improvement in profitability. Using our XYZ Corporation example, with 5,000 customers contributing $500,000 in profits annually through random attraction, we can conservatively estimate that failure to plan our attraction to change the mix over time might cost $100,000 to $150,000 in opportunity per year ($500,000 × 20 to 30 percent). Can you imagine the headline in the local paper if that amount were embezzled from the local franchise — and again the next year, and the next?

Another risk we have to consider is that the competition will find a less expensive way to attract new customers. Dell Computer used direct mail to gain a competitive advantage over Compaq in selling IBM-compatible computers. Land's End and L.L. Bean have thrived with a highly effective, low-cost distribution system. You can buy a car at Sam's Wholesale Club. We can expect it elsewhere.

Let's look at an example in financial services. Merrill Lynch grew its small-business financing unit by 70 percent in 1992 while the banks were flat and declining. This is a large market; in fact, in a *Wall Street Journal* report titled "The Hidden Economy," David Birch estimated that institutional sources (investment banks, commercial banks, and venture capital funds) provide only about 25 percent of the required funds for small business. The remaining 75 percent comes from forgone salaries, second mortgages on homes, friends, relatives, and so on.[9]

Let's assume you are Fidelity Investments or someone with deep pockets, and that you look at the financial services market and decide that the future is small businesses — that you want to be the provider of financial services for them. You look at the profit contribution and you find that the top 5 percent of those small businesses bring in $5,000 each in annual profit to the banks. You see that Merrill Lynch has gained share but, according to the Council on Financial Competition, it costs $5,000 in sales cost to acquire each new customer. That doesn't look so bad, but you ask, "Is there a lower-cost way?" You consider how Dell used a lower-cost sales distribution system.

So here's your plan. You decide to target upper-end small companies — in business more than ten years, and profitable. You use newspaper advertising to attract those who meet your criteria. You offer to match their current bank financing if they will bring all of their business and personal accounts. And you will write them a check for $2,500. You will book it as a loan, but if they stay with you a set number of months and meet certain loan and balance criteria, the loan will be written off. You have cut your sales cost nearly in half. How many small businesses would respond to this offer? We don't know, but the current price wars in other businesses make it likely that this or something like it will occur.

When we move from product focus to customer and market focus, new possibilities open up and the challenge for the local sales-and-service distribution system changes. If we cannot bring unique value through our local unit, we will find ourselves competing with lower-cost delivery mechanisms.

As stewards of a local trade area, it is our job to retain and grow the existing revenue stream. It is also our job to upgrade the mix of customers based on what is available in the trade area. Targeted attraction is a key tool for managing this risk. Failure to compete with increasingly astute businesses for your identified targets would give new meaning to the movie title, *Fatal Attraction*.

There are two risks: one is that our attraction efforts wind up costing too much for the mix of customers we get; the other is that with all the fixed cost, we get no attraction results — we bring in no new customers. Most sales-and-service distribution systems are too expensive not to be bringing in some select new customers. The only thing more expensive than bringing in none is bringing in the wrong ones.

RISK 4: COST

COST RISK IS THE EXPOSURE WE INCUR when the cost of serving and maintaining the customer relationship exceeds the revenue. Unfortunately, for most companies, on well over 20 percent of our customers — and perhaps as many as 30 to 40 percent — we lose money or barely break even. This means that the entire customer base is subsidized by the remaining customers, many of whom are highly profitable. A niche player could serve these high-value customers at a lower price and still remain highly profitable, because it would not be running the race with the same ball and chain that we are — thousands of unprofitable customers. The economics of a branch or store system get miserable pretty fast if we remove the profits of the top 20 percent of our customers but keep their sales and servicing costs. Yet that is exactly what happens frequently in retailing. Full-service stores bear the brunt of educating customers on brands and features, then stand by helplessly as customers make purchases from mail-order or self-serve discounters.

The Cost of Subsidizing the Loss Leaders
How do we assess or quantify this risk? Let's revisit XYZ's 5,000 customers and assume that 20 percent of them are losing us money. That means that 1,000 customers are creating a drag on profitability and that we would be making more if we didn't have to cover their losses. For example, if we are losing $10 or $20 per customer, the overall negative impact is $10,000 to $20,000. We must also realize that, even with their losses, their revenue, however meager, probably does make some contribution to fixed overhead.

Old Strategy:	1,000 unprofitable customers	×	$20 loss	= $ –20,000
New Strategy:	1,000 average customers	×	$100 profit	= $ 100,000
			Net improvement	= **$ 120,000**

Table 5.2. Low-Value Customers Replaced by Average Customers

The real issue is this: What is the cost of using finite sales and service capacity to serve the loss leader? What would that same capacity be worth if aimed at making this group more profitable through fees, minimum purchase requirements, and incentives to capture all of their business? Discounters such as Sam's and Price Club charge this fee on the front end. This fee ensures a way to make money on the lower end, eliminates customers who don't plan to buy, and gains a psychological investment and commitment from the customer. What if those customers who cannot or will not provide revenue to cover their costs were replaced by more profitable customers? Let's look at the possibilities.

Table 5.2 outlines what happens if those 1,000 low-value customers are replaced by 1,000 average customers. This demonstrates a $120,000 risk for not reallocating those resources to higher potential target groups (a 24 percent profit improvement).

Customers			Customer Profitability	Segment Total	
A	500	(10%)	$ 520	$260,000	(52%)
B	1,500	(30%)	$ 80	$120,000	(24%)
C	3,000	(60%)	$ 40	$120,000	(24%)
Total	5,000	(100%)	Average $ 100	Total $500,000	(100%)

10% of the customers = 52% of the profits

Table 5.3. Evaluating and Tiering Customers

Old Strategy:	1,000 unprofitable customers	×	$20 loss	=	$ –20,000
New Strategy:	1,000 best customers	×	$520 profit	=	$ 520,000
			Net improvement	=	**$ 540,000**
			(108% profit improvement)		

Table 5.4. Low-Value Customers Replaced by High-Profit Customers

Now let's look at a more extreme possibility. An objective is set to maximize our return on customer resources. Let's look at two scenarios. First, what if we believe that over two years we can reallocate 20 percent of our time that is currently used for loss leaders, and refocus it to increase the number of A customers.

Suppose that in evaluating and tiering our customers we have found that the distribution looks like table 5.3. This means that the time spent on those 1,000 customers who are losing us $20 each eventually gets reallocated toward serving customers who are making us $520 each. The numbers would look like table 5.4.

Now let's suppose that such a level of success is impossible. What we know is that under this scenario, each 10 percent of replacement or upselling of low-value for high-value customers is worth $54,000 (fig. 5.2). The new A customers may, of course, require more service or a lower price. Even so, there are significant opportunities to enhance the bottom line through small changes in the mix.

Now, before we get totally carried away, let's come back to earth. Just like in the major leagues, no one is going to bat 1.000. In fact, hitting .300 is a major accomplishment.

$ 0   **$ 540,000**

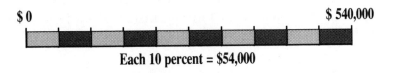

Each 10 percent = $54,000

Figure 5.2. Incremental Value of Upselling

The risk is that by not improving the allocation of cost — the time and effort of our people — by 10 percent, we are probably risking about $54,000 of lost profit per store. By not providing attractive alternatives for moving low-value customers to self service; by spending inordinate amounts of time on the 10 to 20 "service hogs" in each branch or store who use up large amounts of people's time, energy, and empathy; by failing to get fees or minimum purchases from loss leaders — the business incurs real risk. While these customers are getting more than they are paying for, we have highly profitable customers who are being ignored. Dental hygienists are a lower-cost, more efficient way to deliver cleaning services than dentists. We can be no less judicious in managing the cost and value in delivering service to our customers.

Managing this risk requires a way to identify, target, and manage profitability, customer by customer. Much of the sales-and-service productivity problem stems from delivering high-cost, low-value service to unprofitable customers.

It is important to be clear on this point. Are we advising running off our C customers? No! We look for lower-cost ways to meet their needs for service — but at a price that works for them and for us.

Yes, retention, growth, attraction, and cost all represent real risk, the risk that makes a company uncompetitive. And many companies have recognized these risks — one at a time. That's why we keep getting the wave — the program of the month — to deal with the latest risk that has surfaced. Unfortunately, dealing with one risk at a time is like using one finger to plug a dike with many leaks: every time you plug one leak, you open up another. What we need is a strategy that deals simultaneously, market by market, with retention, growth, attraction, and cost management as a comprehensive customer-and-market management system. That is the focus of our next chapter.

6

Managing Market Risk

The Right 4 Strategy

66 Far better an approximate answer to the right question, which is often vague, than an exact answer to the wrong question, which can always be made precise. 99[1]

— *John Tukey, statistician*

*M*ARKET RISK IS REAL. It is quantifiable. Managing it is central to success; failure to do so can put a company or industry out of business. So what are the keys to managing market risk? In emerging industries, new products and technological breakthroughs can play a major role in creating market dominance, and as long as the edge can be maintained, market risk is minimal. In more mature industries, and particularly in mature service-oriented businesses where product or service breakthroughs are relatively rare and easily matched, the primary opportunity for managing market risk is in customer sales and service. Accordingly, the primary mission of the sales-and-service delivery system is to manage market risk.

Competing airlines fly people on planes made by the same manufacturers, land and take off at the same airports, share reservation systems, and have meals prepared by the same food service companies. Competing retail stores have much of the same merchandise, are often located in close proximity — even in the same malls, with similar hours. The same is true in insurance, fast food, grocery, and many other industries.

More and more, the battle gets waged at the point of sales and service. Producers of food products are acutely aware of this shift in focus as they fight for shelf space, promotion, and merchandising advantage in grocery stores.

Let's take a closer look at the challenge facing airlines. In 1992, the airlines lost $2 billion, yet their primary sales-and-service distribution arm, the travel agents, continues to grow and prosper. According to a *Wall Street Journal* article:

> A decade ago, 15,000 travel agencies sold only 40 percent of all airline tickets. Today, the nation's 32,000 agencies handle 85 percent of airline business. But the cost of that service has risen faster than any other airline expense. In 1992, airlines paid

travel agents $5.3 billion, up 9 percent from 1991 and more than 300 percent since 1978, according to Airline Reporting Corporation. . . . Once a small item on airline accounting sheets, commissions are now the industry's third largest expense, behind only labor and fuel.[2]

Think of it! Getting your airline reservation costs you more than your share of the plane. Last year travel agency commissions rose twice as fast as airline revenues in percentage terms.

Why is this happening to an industry under siege? The power has shifted to the distribution side of the business, while the product, air travel, has become a commodity. What happens if the airlines do not respond to the demands of the travel agents? Ask People Express. Airline officials say it collapsed in part because agents steered business travelers away from it. At a time when the airlines need desperately to control their costs, they have lost control of their distribution system and their costs are going up. They cannot rein in the costs for fear of losing revenue and customers.

In many businesses our primary opportunity to please or displease the market comes down to customer sales-and-service management: how we target, create, maintain, and sustain customers. We can refer to this as our "customer factory." The mission of the customer factory is to design, engineer, and manufacture profitable customer relationships based on value. As we extend our manufacturing analogy, we begin to see that there are certain questions we must answer if we are to compete. What are we here to manufacture? How much? With what? From what raw material? At what cost and what price? Should we produce only one thing, or should we have the capability to produce several things?

All of these are basic questions that must be answered, whether we are producing widgets or customers. Getting the answers right creates opportunity. Getting them wrong creates risk.

THE RIGHT 4

IN A PROFITABLE CUSTOMER-MANAGEMENT FACTORY, there are four things that we must get right:

1. Right sales
2. Right service
3. Right customer/markets
4. Right cost

Figure 6.1 shows one way to look at the four paramount objectives of a market-driven customer culture. An effective market-driven customer factory must get all these objectives right, tie them together, and align them to work together. The reason many companies went through the sales, service, and cost containment waves was to break the problem into smaller chunks and focus on a single key risk; a worthy objective, but often done in a way that neglected or exacerbated other problems. There was no strategic connectivity.

Let's look at these objectives one at a time.

1. Sales and sales management: Managing the right sales efforts and results. During this wave many businesses attracted new customers and cross-sold existing customers. But in many cases service levels slipped, costs were too high, and they did not target the right markets.

2. Service and service management: Delivering the right service levels. "Service wars" significantly enhanced service quality. However, in many cases, time and attention on sales went down, as did results. Service delivered indiscriminately to unprofitable customers further increased costs and drove out service enhancements for our best customers, many of whom paid for and expected "best service" but ended up being ignored.

3. Cost containment: Selling and servicing at the right cost. When we made cost reduction the "program of the month," we were able to get costs down. Unfortunately, when sales and service declined as

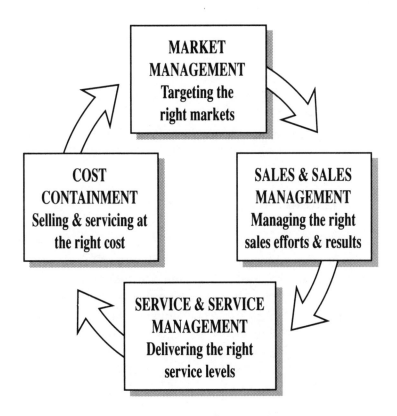

© 1993 ActionSystems Inc., Dallas, Texas

Figure 6.1. Market-Driven Customer Culture

well, we did not get the lasting margins we had hoped for because we did not improve productivity. Exacerbating the problem was the fact that we did not reduce costs in the right segments (loss leaders); thus, we neglected some of our best customers while they were being wooed by the competition.

4. Market management: Targeting the right markets. Customers and markets were often targeted by a centralized micromarketing function, with little translation into specific sales, service, and cost practices for each local branch or store. Advertising, product development, direct mail, and other activities were not directed or tailored to the best opportunities in local trade areas.

The goal is to get all four objectives right at the same time — sales, service, costs, and markets. The risk of getting them wrong is obvious. And the need to reduce them to manageable tasks makes sense, but not at the expense of effectiveness. What strategy accomplishes this objective, so that we manage the risk and seize the opportunity?

REENGINEERING SALES AND SERVICE

TO MEET OUR OBJECTIVE, WE NEED TO THINK of our customers and prospects in terms of their needs, their willingness to pay, and their potential. Ultimately we must define sales-and-service delivery alternatives that match customer requirements. As market managers, we are faced with the same challenge as plant managers. What are the service delivery levels we must reengineer to create the desired output: profitable customers? For discussion purposes, let's assume three different levels of sales and service: transaction, multiproduct, and account management (table 6.1).

Transaction service: Basic order taking and routine transactions. The objective of this activity, for both the customer and the organization, is quick, efficient and low-cost service. Customers know what they want and the company dispenses it, typically through self-service mechanisms, tellers, clerks, or customer service representatives. There is virtually no advice or consultation involved; nor is there tailoring of the product or its delivery, both of which are standard. The focus is on gathering accounting and administrative information to consummate the purchase — no more. Staff people are assigned not to customers but to transactions. Typical examples are basic cash withdrawals from banks, self-service gasoline, self-help discount stores, and 1-800 telephone purchases.

Multiproduct service: Giving customers the opportunity to discuss needs without knowing exactly which product to ask for. Here the

	Account Management	Multi-Product	Transaction
Delivery Level	Value-added service Consolidation of relationships Large-ticket sales	Cross-selling Cultivation of high potentials Promotion of targeted products	Low-cost transactions Efficient service Referrals
Skills:			
Existing clients	Relationship orientation Expanding relationships Advanced product skills Negotiation	Selling on demand Handling complaints Basic product skills Recognition of high potentials	Handling routine transactions Handling complaints Making referrals
New clients	Referrals Prospecting	Direct mail Telemarketing	Direct mail Advertising

© *1993 ActionSystems Inc., Dallas, Texas*

Table 6.1. Three Levels of Service

customer gets assistance in determining which product or products best meet his or her identified need(s). In some cases, the discussion will reveal other needs, so multiproduct service brings both help in decision-making and a broader array of products or services to the buying process. The company gets an opportunity to cross-sell and upsell the client while assessing the potential for future business with the customer. A salesperson is assigned to identify what the customer needs, help the customer make the right selection, and consummate the purchase. The staff person's assignment is only for the duration of the customer's visit or interaction. However, this additional help adds cost that usually is offset by either higher prices or greater volume. Examples include a waiter in a restaurant, a new-accounts person in a bank, a salesperson in a department store, and a service representative in an auto repair shop.

Account management service: Proactive consultation and advice. In this type of service, the client's needs and/or potential are such that he or she is assigned a representative, an account manager, by the company. This representative personally contacts the client and adds service value by acquiring background information on the client, evaluating the client's needs, helping make buying decisions, and suggesting other purchases. Advice and consultation are a key part of the relationship.

The company representative manages the client both when he or she is present and when he or she is absent. Examples include a personal physician, a private or personal banker, and a national account sales representative. Because this level of personal service is expensive, the company must collect enough revenue or usage fees to ensure that it is profitable.

More than one of these levels of service may be needed in a given branch or store. In smaller units, one person may have to perform several roles — personal banker for Mrs. Smith; multiproduct, new-account representative for Mr. Jones. In some cases, the sales-and-service function may be integrated; in others, separated (the insurance industry has been a leader in separating sales from processing, service, and underwriting). Distribution channels (store, telephone, computer, or fax) may be single or multiple.

Just as the effective plant manager in today's manufacturing world must be looking for ways to reengineer process to create greater efficiency and output, so must the market manager look for ways to reengineer service delivery to bring better value to customers and shareholders. Most experts see this emphasis emerging already in some industries. According to *The Wall Street Journal*, many banks are focused on gaining these efficiencies in their administrative processing:

> Reengineering appears to be progressing most rapidly in banking. Banc One, PNC Financial Corporation, First Bank System Inc., NationsBank, and many others are scrambling to streamline their back-office operations. Waino Pihl, a partner in Andersen Consulting's banking practice, predicts that reengineering will reduce employment in commercial banks and thrift institutions by 30 to 40 percent over the next seven years.[3]

The same commitment and rigor are needed on the sales-and-service side of the business. How do we make our sales and service four or five times more productive? We must systematically evaluate opportunities to lower cost and enhance revenue by making informed decisions on our sales and service.

MANAGING YOUR A'S, B'S, AND C'S

IN PRACTICE, OF COURSE, our "three levels of service" are not distinct but form a continuum. But within this continuum, how do we assign or allocate service levels to customers based on their needs and willingness to pay?

Let's again assume three levels of customers: A's, B's, and C's. As we think of these groups, we must consider the business they have with us and the corresponding contributions to the organization's overhead and profits. We can call this their *current value*, and the future business they might have with us is their *potential value*. Our first cut will usually be based on current value.

"A" customers: Top customers, based on current or potential profit contribution to the organization. These customers tend to have more complex needs or be more discerning users of service. They are often willing to pay for value-added assistance in meeting those needs — in either price, volume, referral, or loyalty. In the airline industry, these may be first-class fliers, who pay for better service, or frequent fliers who fly hundreds of thousands of coach-class miles each year. In hotels and car rental businesses, they may be certain repeat business travelers. In banks, they may be retail customers who contribute over $1,000 in annual profits. Across virtually all industries, this market segment contributes close to half an organization's profits and is heavily chased by the competition.

"B" customers: Midmarket customers for whom less added value appears warranted, either because needs are less significant or because willingness to pay is diminished. This group's current or potential value to the company is in the midrange. Some of these

customers are "migrating up" — that is, their potential needs and value will eventually make them A customers. Others look like B's, based on our share of their business, but would be A's if we had all their business. Some are permanent B's, but make a significant contribution to the organization's profits.

"C" customers: Lowest-profit customers, based on current contributions. Most research tells us that, the way we now manage these customers, we lose money or barely break even on 20 to 30 percent of them. Some businesses, however, by lowering costs or imposing front-end fees, serve nearly all their C customers profitably. However, even if we lose money on C's with and without potential — that is, our costs exceed our revenues — their business offsets some of our overhead. Many of these customers, but not all, tend to be our lowest in either complexity of needs or willingness to pay. In local trade areas where C customers make up virtually all the market, we can run a very profitable branch or store *if* we manage our costs effectively.

Although these categories help us generalize about needs, there are many exceptions. Some of our most sophisticated customers, for example, may also be very demanding when it comes to willingness to pay. Different target groups within a market segment may also have very different needs and buying motives. For instance, the needs and willingness to pay of first-class fliers and frequent coach fliers may be quite different, even though both are A customers.

MATCHING SERVICE LEVELS AND CUSTOMER VALUE

THUS WE HAVE ARBITRARILY DESIGNATED three groups of customers, tiered according to current or potential contribution to the business; and we have specified three levels of service based on customer needs and their willingness to pay (in your company, there could be more or fewer). The question is, how do we align customer levels and service levels both to meet customer needs and to make a profit? In the process, how do we minimize the retention, growth, attraction, and cost risks discussed in chapter 5?

The effectiveness of any sales-and-service system is tied directly to its ability to deliver the right sales with the right service to the right customers at the right cost. Choices must be made. If we are a niche player, we may have pursued a strategy of serving only A's or C's, and provided only account management or transaction service. But in a dynamic market we may have to reevaluate that decision. Although already successful as a discounter, Wal-Mart created the super-discount Sam's Club to go after small businesses, institutions, large families, and other volume discount buyers. Many self-service gas stations have now moved to card-operated gas pumps, eliminating the need for a customer-cashier interaction of any kind. These decisions must be constantly revisited by the company and applied, tailored, and refined locally by market managers. For example, markets with high concentrations of affluent, widowed, female senior citizens may find card-operated, self-service gas stations a challenge.

To make these decisions, we must be able to answer certain questions about our customer factory. Who are our A's, B's, and C's? How many of each are in our trade area? How many of each do we have as customers? How many would we like to have? How would we choose to change the mix? How many levels of service do they want or need? How many levels of service do we provide? How are we currently applying these service levels to our A's, B's, and C's? How well do these levels stack up competitively? Who are our high-potential customers and prospects?

Value Gaps

As we address these questions, we begin to identify gaps in our local sales and service. Where are we too expensive, delivering more service than the customer is willing to pay for? Where are we underdelivering servicing, giving them less than they want or have paid for? What parts of our customer segments are at risk? What customer groups are we currently attracting? (High value? Loss leaders? Don't know?) What opportunities are we missing with our high-potential customers?

MARKET SEGMENTS	DELIVERY LEVELS		
	Account Management	Multi-Product	Transaction
A Customers			
B Customers			
C Customers			

© 1993 ActionSystems Inc., Dallas, Texas

Figure 6.2. Sales-and-Service Delivery Levels

The difference between store or branch managers and market managers is that market managers eat these questions for breakfast. They are riveted on profitably winning the marketplace. While store managers and branch managers focus on running the store or branch, market managers focus on winning the market.

We need to align service levels against market segments in order to assess our effectiveness, and identify the gaps so we can manage the risk. Let's begin by creating a Market Segment–Service Delivery map. Figure 6.2 helps us look at allocation of sales and service to customers within market segments.

RETENTION: THE RISK OF UNDERDELIVERY

IF WE START WITH OUR A CUSTOMERS, we may quickly find that if they are getting transaction service it does not meet their complex needs nor deliver the value they are paying for. For their contribution to the company, they should be receiving "Cadillac" service. That's what they need and are willing to pay for. Yet many are getting only "Chevrolets" — in some cases, previously owned. If we can't give them a higher level of service, then we had better offer them a lower price — before the competition does. The unpardonable sin is not delivering value. These value gaps lead to retention risk, in the form of either lost customers or the loss of some of their profitable business (fig. 6.3).

Likewise, we have B customers who get transaction service but have additional needs. Like A customers, they are paying for more service than they are receiving. They should be able to get a broader array of products and services (one-stop shopping) and some assistance in addressing additional needs. If we don't fulfill these

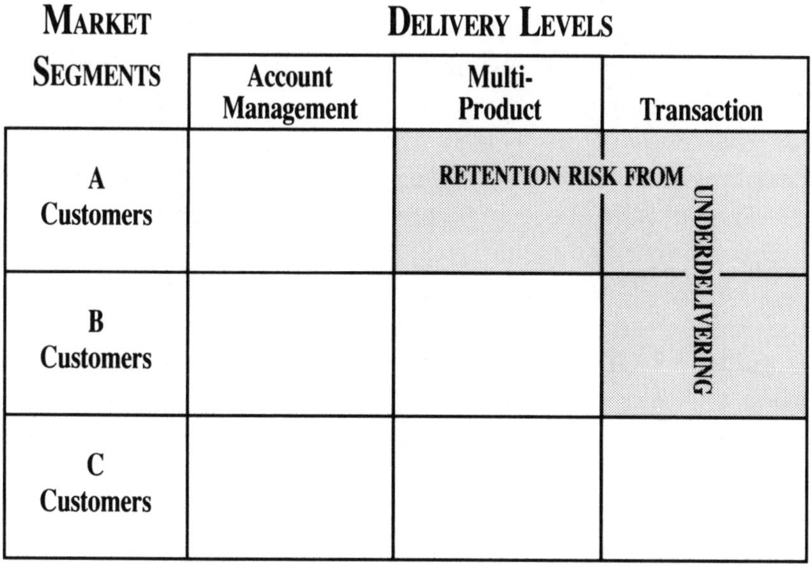

MARKET SEGMENTS	DELIVERY LEVELS		
	Account Management	Multi-Product	Transaction
A Customers		RETENTION RISK FROM	
B Customers			UNDERDELIVERING
C Customers			

(Shaded areas represent risk areas to avoid.)

© *1993 ActionSystems Inc., Dallas, Texas*

Figure 6.3. Sales-and-Service Delivery: Risk of Underdelivering

needs, our B customers may buy from other stores, through the mail, in response to telephone solicitation, or by other means.

Many businesses have set up preferred-client, frequent-flier, gold-service, or other programs to manage the risk, especially for their A customers. While some of these programs have worked well, others have been less successful. Marketing promotions have often advertised benefits that were not delivered locally. Many banks promised a personal banker for their better customers, but failed to give them differentiated, personalized service. Delivering high-value products with low-value or no-value service is a good way to create customer-retention risk.

COST: THE RISK OF OVERDELIVERY

NOW LET'S LOOK AT THE OTHER END OF THE SPECTRUM. If our C customers are getting time and attention because they are friends of the staff or because they come in frequently with many demands, we are delivering more service and sales to them than their balances, fees, sales, and referrals warrant (fig. 6.4). We are giving Cadillacs to people who may be paying us only for Chevrolets. Besides, if their needs are not complex, our service attention may provide them only marginal value.

Our expense risk from overdelivering is in direct conflict with our Right 4 strategy. Someone has to pay for this overdelivery. Unfortunately, it's usually our best customers who subsidize our loss leaders. If our niche competitors "cherry pick" — steal them away by offering a better deal — we lose their profits, their subsidies, and their contributions to overhead. Then we are faced with another choice: either the shareholders (or owners) fund the loss through reduced profits, or the business lowers its cost — for example, by laying off employees. There is no free lunch; someone must pay.

When we conduct training sessions on sales and service, we often ask first- and second-line managers which of these two risks, the retention risk of underdelivery to A customers or the expense

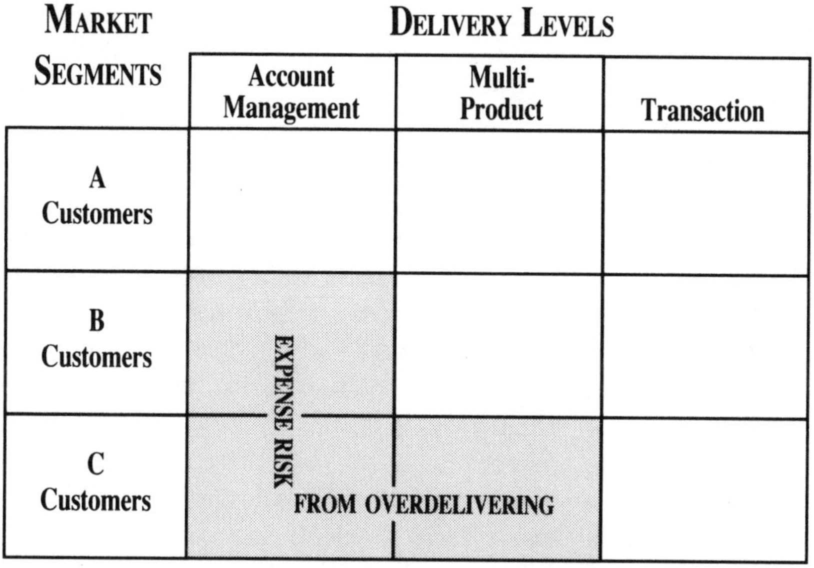

MARKET SEGMENTS	DELIVERY LEVELS		
	Account Management	Multi-Product	Transaction
A Customers			
B Customers	EXPENSE RISK		
C Customers	FROM OVERDELIVERING		

(Shaded areas represent risk areas to avoid.)

© *1993 ActionSystems Inc., Dallas, Texas*

Figure 6.4. Sales-and-Service Delivery: Risk of Overdelivering

risk of overdelivery to C customers, is of greater concern to them. They are often split as to which is their primary pain.

Managing Retention and Cost: Staying on the Diagonal

This takes us to the heart of the problem. Many companies have recognized the need to better manage their best customers, and have set up initiatives to do so. Yet they have been less successful than they expected. Why? Because focusing on A customers doesn't work very well when people are so busy reacting to a flood of C customers that they have no time — especially in a service culture where a customer's letter of complaint to the chairman creates real grief.

Our people are so busy avoiding complaints and ensuring that in-branch/in-store service is "legendary" that they have no time to get to A customers. This is particularly a problem for department stores, banks, and other businesses where certain A customers make fewer visits to the premises. A growing challenge for the market manager is maintaining mind share and access. When we implement an initiative to be more proactive in contacting and servicing A's without streamlining and freeing up service capacity from the C's, we create a no-win situation. No wonder sales training did not lead to more selling. No wonder our people are stressed — they don't know how to do both. No wonder we are disappointed with service initiatives where customer satisfaction has improved but customer retention and share of wallet are headed south. We have done nothing to handle that 800-pound gorilla, branch or store traffic, that is getting in the way.

This leads to another challenge. Many companies have put heavy emphasis on cross-selling. Through sales training and other initiatives, they have asked their people to cross-sell anything that moves. But if our predominant traffic is C customers, we are expending our most valuable resource, our people's time and expertise, against the market segment with the least need. It is not surprising that we have been disappointed in the results: high-cost efforts with low value contribution to both the customer and the company.

There are three losers in the game the way it is often played. Our A customers lose by not getting their needs met. Our staff lose because they go home feeling like failures at the end of the work day. The company loses the most valuable part of its franchise, its high-value customers. In fact, it may be exchanging high-value customers for high-cost, low-profit customers.

While many companies have dramatically cut costs, most have failed to change the way they do business. For example, in cutting costs without reallocating staff time, they have simply gotten smaller. They have done nothing to improve margins or productivity. Cost cutting that runs off the best customers will sharply decrease productivity over time. Cost is not the problem! Productivity and margins are the problem.

The solution, in terms of our diagram, is to manage along the diagonal (fig. 6.5). We must become very purposeful about basing

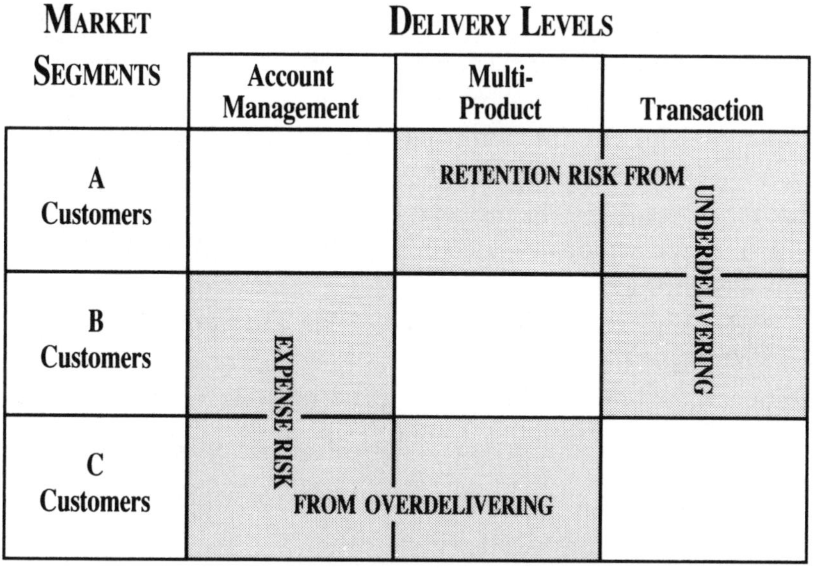

MARKET SEGMENTS	DELIVERY LEVELS		
	Account Management	Multi-Product	Transaction
A Customers		RETENTION RISK FROM	UNDERDELIVERING
B Customers	EXPENSE RISK		
C Customers	FROM OVERDELIVERING		

(Which target groups fall into the unshaded boxes?)

©1993 ActionSystems Inc., Dallas, Texas

Figure 6.5. Sales-and-Service Delivery: Balance

our allocations of staff and other resources on customer and organizational needs. A sales-and-service strategy that does not factor in cost cannot be successful in today's world. Like airbags, diet cola, frequent-flier programs, cable television, fax machines, and other innovations, we must meet the needs of the 20th century. We have to perform the basics, but in a smarter, more focused way: installing a customer strategy that matches sales and service with market segments.

GROWTH: THE RISK OF UNDERSELLING

WE MUST BE CONCERNED WITH MORE than just retention and cost. The third variable has to do with our high-potential customers — some of whom are high value and some not.

Let's start with the C's. We know, based on current profitability, that some of our customers who appear to be C's are really A-type customers in total contributions to us and our competitors. Unfortunately, we just don't have much of their business; they would be very profitable if we had all or most of it. We also know that there are others who are currently C's, but when they get out of college, or when the estate is finalized, will become B's or A's. Others will always be C's.

Conventional wisdom has always been to let our least-skilled staff handle the C customer. However, to optimize value to the customer and profits to the company, we must do three things well:

1. Provide highly efficient, low-cost service or transactions.
2. Establish minimum fees for services for which revenues do not cover costs.
3. Identify cross-sell opportunities and refer customers who are "move-up" candidates.

Our front-line people need special skills in order to be efficient and productive in identifying referral and upgrade possibilities.

Identifying upgrade candidates is a crucial part of the Right 4 strategy. Since they are already customers and we know something about them, our cost of sales for getting additional business from them is potentially lower than for a new prospect. Studies have shown that it costs five times as much to acquire business from a new customer as from an existing customer.[4]

The same goes for our B and A customers, because we seldom have all their business. Here the risk increases that our competitors will out-position us for their business.

This growth strategy is an essential part of our customer management system. We can plot this opportunity on our chart (fig. 6.6).

Growth requires being very proactive in cross-selling and upselling. As market managers, we must specify where the growth potential exists in the local trade area: young couples, business executives, families with small children, and customers of certain competitors. For business-to-business potential, we must specify

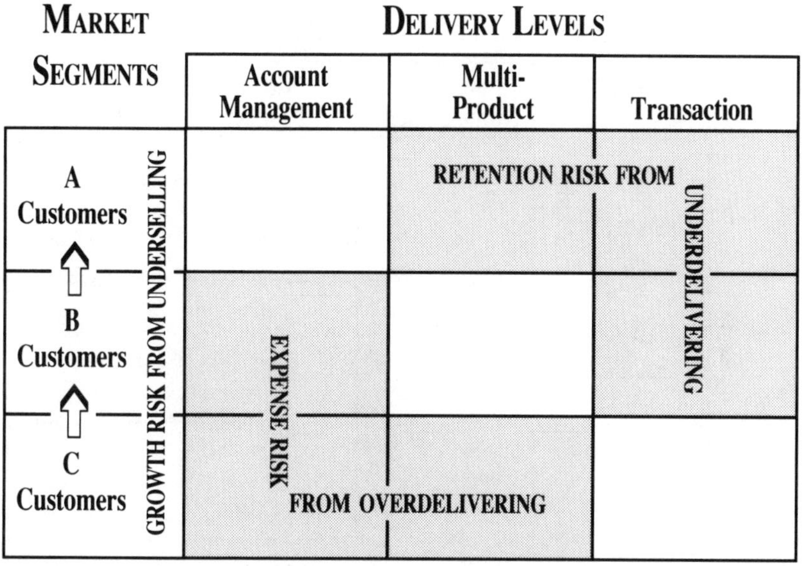

MARKET SEGMENTS	DELIVERY LEVELS		
	Account Management	Multi-Product	Transaction
A Customers ⇧	GROWTH RISK FROM UNDERSELLING	RETENTION RISK FROM UNDERDELIVERING	
B Customers ⇧			
C Customers	EXPENSE RISK FROM OVERDELIVERING		

© 1993 ActionSystems Inc., Dallas, Texas

Figure 6.6. Sales-and-Service Delivery: Risk of Underselling

company sizes, types of industry, and regions. As with retention, this most often means we must free up time and capacity from some of our C customers in order to carry it off.

ATTRACTION: THE RISK OF POOR TARGETING

TO AVOID ESTABLISHING AN UNDESIRABLE CUSTOMER MIX, sales-and-service managers should address certain questions before planning efforts or campaigns to attract new business. What is the profit potential of the new customers you are acquiring? What are your acquisition costs? Do you have the resources to attract the most desirable market segments? Finding time to prospect is not easy, nor is it, in many markets, the best use of your time. However, failure to

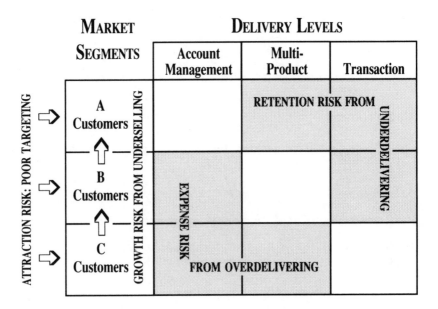

© 1993 ActionSystems Inc., Dallas, Texas

Figure 6.7. Sales-and-Service Delivery: Risk of Poor Targeting

go after certain types of prospects may lower the quality of your customer mix (fig. 6.7).

You know that each year your local unit will lose a certain percentage of its customers to relocation, death, and competitive encroachment. The questions are these: What type of customer is currently coming to you to replace those losses? What is the profile of the type(s) that you are seeking in the local trade area? How many resources are being used to get them? In some local markets you need an overall gain in number of customers. In other markets you have heavy market share, but need to increase your percentage of profitable customers by replacing lost customers with more select customers. There are local trade areas where profitability can be increased by reducing the number of customers overall while changing the mix of A's, B's, and C's. For example, our consultants saw one small business banking center decrease its market share from 41 to 38 percent while increasing profitability by 15 percent. In most markets, however, your best strategy is to retain or grow share while enhancing the mix. Decisions on allocating attraction time and effort must be based on the total client mix as well as the local market potential.

One of the toughest problems facing a local franchise is having a mix of customers, attracted over a period of time, that sub-optimizes the return from the trade area. Once this mix has become established, changing to a more profitable set of customers may be as challenging as starting a new customer base from scratch.

MARKET MANAGERS ADDRESS THE MARKET

TO IMPROVE THE COMPANY'S MIX OF CUSTOMERS, simply managing sales and service while holding the line on cost is not enough. An effective sales-and-service system must be composed of market managers who can tailor the different strategies of retention, growth, attraction, and cost management to specific groups within A, B, and C market segments, and who will provide transaction, multiproduct, and account management services to specific groups of customers and prospects in a trade area based on need, contribution, potential, and willingness to pay.

What is the difference between store or branch managers and market managers? Store managers focus on what is going on inside the store. Market managers see the store as one means or one channel for profitably winning the battle for the market. Store managers manage the noise; market managers manage the market.

These market managers are, first and last, heatseekers. They prepare their game plan for the local trade area by focusing on high-gain activities. Their map for winning local markets includes these key elements:

- *Objective* — right sales, right service, right markets, right cost
- *Key strategies* — retention, growth, attraction, cost
- *Market segments* — A's, B's, C's, and target groups with similar buying motives

■ *Sales-and-service levels* — transaction, multiproduct, account management

Market managers know that the objectives, key strategies, markets, and sales-and-service levels must work together — that focusing on strategy alone, without considering different markets and appropriate service levels, will create chaos, confusion, and poor results. However, a coherent sales-and-service strategy enables the local market manager to operate at a higher level, with specific answers to these questions:

■ Where are we too expensive?
■ Where are we underdelivering?
■ What parts of our customer segments are at risk?
■ What customer groups are we currently attracting?
■ What opportunities are we missing with our high-potential customers?

As much as we would like to have standard answers to these questions, the ability to optimize local market potential means that these questions have very different answers market by market.

THE POWER OF A SPECIFIC VISION

BILL RUSSELL, A FORMER BOSTON CELTIC and perhaps the best defensive basketball player in NBA history, said that as he approached each game, he focused on the player he would be guarding. He would consider the number of points the player was averaging per game and visualize his strengths and weaknesses. He said:

> My goal was always to hold him to one-half of his scoring average by taking away his two best moves to the basket. If he was going to exceed one-half of his scoring average, he would have to do it with his third- and fourth-best moves.

It is that level of specificity that must be applied against the unique market potential and competition in a local market.

Sales-and-Service Strategy	Market-Driven Sales-and-Service Strategy
Improve retention by improving service	Improve retention of "franchise customers" by providing service levels that remove defection risk
Increase cross-sell efforts	Increase cross-sell efforts to those customers for whom the expected return exceeds the costs (convert high potentials; know whom not to cross-sell)
Reduce costs	Reduce costs of serving C customers through appropriate delivery systems
Increase in-branch/ store service levels	Target service enhancement for highly profitable customers who seldom come into the branch/store
Attract competitor's customers	Attract competitor's "franchise customers" and high-potential customers
Increase market share	Increase market share of profitable customer groups

©1993 ActionSystems Inc., Dallas, Texas

Table 6.2. Transitioning from Sales Culture to Market Culture

In order for front-line people to begin to shift from a sales-and-service culture to a market culture, the business owner or executive in charge must define a more specific vision with a higher level of productivity and payoff. For some, tired of the jargon of "vision" as a leadership concept, it simply boils down to *intention*. What is our intention when it comes to making our sales-and-service delivery system more productive? What does the intended shift look like? Table 6.2 summarizes this shift.

So if an integrated market-driven culture is required to manage our risks and leverage our opportunities, how do we get there market by market? The third part of this book deals with three key principles that provide a foundation for getting there. Part IV will deal with the key practices and cultural-change issues that are key to implementation.

PART

III

THE
BREAKOUT
PERFORMER

*Three
Key Principles*

these elements to profitably win our local market?

When companies excel at delivering value, the results can be startling. Wal-Mart produces 50 percent more revenue per square foot than its competitors;[1] Southwest Airlines handles nearly three times as many passengers per employee as some of its competitors.[2]

Scoreboards and standings tell us clearly that some teams play much better than others. Yet no matter how closely we watch the scores, they tell us little about what happens on the practice field, in the trenches, in preparation of the game plan, and in coaching sessions to produce the results. Looking at the finished painting tells the untrained eye very little about how the artist created it.

My colleagues and I have spent the past 14 years training with and analyzing the success of top performers in local branches, stores, and centers to understand how they manage sales, service, customers/markets, and costs. We have also worked extensively with mediocre and marginal performers. We have observed that top per-

*T*his part of the book deals with how to become a breakout performer by implementing the Right 4 — right sales, right service, right customers, at the right cost. We know that retention, growth, attraction, and cost management are the key elements of the Streetcorner Strategy. The question is, How do we apply

formers do certain things that less successful performers are not willing to do or are doing poorly.

Pat Riley, NBA coach of the decade and now coach of the New York Knicks, was asked by a reporter after earning one of his NBA championships about the key to his success. Riley responded that his team "did all of the same things that other teams did — but perhaps did them just a little better." The reporter persisted: "But that sounds so simple." With the veins in his neck bulging, Riley retorted, "Oh, it's simple — *but it is not easy!*"

It is not *easy* to address the factors that lead to sustained success. And sure enough, about the time we think we have them figured out, the market, the competition, the rate environment, the technology, or something else changes. If we are looking for breakout performance, we must define the general guidelines or principles that produce success in an ever-changing marketplace.

In our attempts to look beyond results and into root causes, we have found three key strategic principles that provide advantage, if not breakout performance, in running a branch or store system: acting local, segmenting the market, and achieving breakthrough productivity. These principles are simple — but they are not easy.

7

Acting Local

A More Productive Strategy

> **"** Think
> Global —
> Act Local. **"** [1]
>
> — *Theodore Levitt*

*I*N HIS AUTOBIOGRAPHY, *MADE IN AMERICA*, Sam Walton identified his first principle of retailing: "Think one store at a time." He illustrates it this way:

> We've got one store in Panama City, Florida, and another only five miles away in Panama City Beach, but actually they're worlds apart when it comes to their merchandise mix and their customer base. They're entirely different kinds of stores. One is built for tourists going to the beach and the other is more like the normal Wal-Mart, built for folks who live in town. . . . Focusing on a single store can accomplish a number of things. First, of course, it enables us to actually improve that store. But if in the process we also happen to learn a particular way in which that Panama City Beach Wal-Mart is outsmarting the competition on, say, beach towels, then we can quickly get that information out to all our other beach stores around the country and see if their approach works everywhere.[2]

David Glass, CEO of Wal-Mart, elaborates from an executive management perspective:

> I don't know any other large retail company — Kmart, Sears, Penney's — that discusses their sales at the end of the week in any smaller breakdown than by region. We talk about individual stores.[3]

All of this from a corporation whose financial performance looks like table 7.1 over the past 30 years.

THE POWER OF THINKING SMALL

THE PRINCIPLE OF "ACTING LOCAL" simply means that much of winning or losing is determined by the local people, competing against local competitors for local customers and prospects. Research confirms again and again, in service-oriented businesses, that much of the variability of sales, service, costs, and margins is determined by local capability.

	1960	1970	1980	1990
Sales	$1.4 million	$31 million	$1.2 billion	$26 billion
Profits	$112,000	$1.2 million	$41 million	$1 billion
Stores	9	32	276	1,528

Adapted from a chart found in Sam Walton's book, Made in America

Table 7.1. Wal-Mart's Financial Performance

Acting local does not mean making all decisions locally. Many are best made and executed in the head office. Economies of scale, organization-wide strategy, and minimization of duplication are just a few of the issues that support central decisions. Too often, however, businesses fail to apply, tailor, and implement those decisions flexibly and purposefully in the local trade area.

And Wal-Mart is not alone. The Royal Bank of Canada, the third-largest bank in North America, with more than 1,600 branches, 7.5 million customers, and a 1991 income of nearly $1 billion, has instituted a plan to be "small and local." In the September–October 1991 *Harvard Business Review*, Ram Charan described it this way:

> Indeed, the plan could have been a primer on translating the abstract rhetoric of "empowerment" into tangible management principles. It emphasized the importance of personalized leadership by area managers, local market intelligence, interactive planning driven by the field, and local autonomy to provide area managers with the flexibility they needed.[4]

Xerox Corporation is also experimenting with a strategy of changing from rigid corporate hierarchy to local flexibility. Arizona is one of two areas where it will be piloted. The 280-employee Arizona district can now make its own decisions about customer service, financing terms, advertising, employees, and other matters that it used to refer to headquarters.

David Myerscough, senior vice president of U.S. customer operations for Xerox, compared the "Leap-Out" plan to having locally managed franchises under the oversight of corporate quality control, like McDonald's restaurants:

> If I am going to be quick and decisive and get to the market in a competitive manner, I need to create something like Xerox franchises throughout the United States.... We want to have the advantages of a big corporation without the disadvantages of bigness. We'll get decisions made quicker and, equally important, we'll retain our better people. We can still give them the security a big company offers, but with the fun and excitement they'd have in a little company.[5]

Why is the principle of acting local so important? Is it another one of those "do-good," soft, empowerment things that is long on lofty, uplifting promises but short on reality in a very tough business world? We believe not. We identify three key reasons why acting local is a principle that customers require and that companies must master.

REASON 1: MARKET DIVERSITY

THE CONCEPT OF LOCAL MARKET UNIQUENESS IS NOT NEW. Every local manager has claimed that his market is unique. Often, this claim is used as a reason to resist head office initiatives. But, the fact is, local markets *are* different.

Different Strokes for Different Folks

Why act local? It's simple: "Give the customers what they want." Old vs. young, rich vs. poor, working vs. retired, ethnic vs. nonethnic, urban vs. rural, indigenous vs. transient — all want different things. Within the mission of the organization, market managers must discover what their target groups want.

When Food Lion, Inc., with 938 grocery stores, planned a rapid expansion in the Dallas–Fort Worth area, retail consultants John

Small and David Mills, with Strategic Retail Consulting, were charged with the task of plotting 42 suburban store locations. As reported by Pat Baldwin in *The Dallas Morning News:*

> The strategy of the aggressive, low-price supermarket chain immediately became clear. . . . The well-publicized, much-anticipated "store wars" actually would crystallize as guerrilla warfare — localized skirmishes. . . . "While there is a tendency for marketers to look at Dallas-Forth Worth as a single market," Mr. Small said, "groceries are sold in *neighborhoods*." In other words, the Food Lion battleground focuses on neighborhood competition within about a 5-mile radius.[6]

In assessing the results a year later, most observers concluded that the opening of 42 stores resulted in performance that was "tamer than expected." Three key reasons are cited for Food Lion's challenges (prior to ABC's "20/20" news show on food-handling practices). One, their reputation as a low-cost/low-price grocery chain caused many local stores to lower their prices in anticipation of Food Lion pricing. A lot of their competitive differentiation was diluted. Two, although about 75 percent of their stores are reputed to be doing well, 25 percent of the stores are contributing below expectations — they are not winning their local markets. Three, the Southwest is different from the Southeast. Ron Johnston, associate publisher of the *Shelby Report*, an industry trade publication based in Gainesville, Georgia, believes Food Lion

> not only underestimated the fervor of Dallas–Fort Worth competition, but also the upscale shopping expectations of consumers. They made some assumptions about consumers in the Southwest; they are different from consumers in the Southeast. Dallas, in particular, is a market noted for its upscale consumer demographics and high disposable income rates. That translates into a taste favoring brand names.[7]

It also means that appearance, ambience and in-store service are important. During this key market initiative for Food Lion, at least one local competitor introduced valet parking in one of its affluent markets.

Who Decides What? (Central vs. Local Decisions)

McDonald's, often identified as the quintessential model for consistency and simplicity, continues to reevaluate central vs. local decisions. Although they have established a clear international brand identity with certain things standardized (Big Mac, Egg McMuffin, Golden Arches), they have also emphasized local initiatives. Suburban locations often provide large playgrounds, double-window drive-throughs, and lots of children's birthday parties on Saturdays. Downtown locations may offer none of these. You can get sushi at McDonald's in Vancouver, a *Wall Street Journal* with your Big Mac and fries in New York's Wall Street district — and soon, beefless burgers in India, a market of a mere 844 million potential customers. Yet no McDonald's has ever become an expensive, white-table restaurant. All these examples illustrate one idea: We are here to serve customers, and their pattern of needs varies across markets.

American Airlines and Delta Air Lines fight it out — and a lot of the battle is over local issues. In Dallas, American's local campaign "Based Here, Best Here" stressed being headquartered in Dallas with a workforce of more than 26,000 people, while drawing attention implicitly to its size and number of flights. Delta countered that local initiative with its "Easy Street," promoting the ease of its one-terminal access compared to huge, two-terminal American, where you may end up parked in a different terminal 20 to 30 minutes away from your return gate. American has since installed a convenient, direct-access tram, at considerable cost, that cuts travel time between its two terminals. And the local battle goes on.

Companies must decide what is negotiable locally and what is not. Which decisions must be made centrally and not market by market? These "non-negotiables" are what Bob Lane, president of NationsBank Texas, calls the "by Gods": "By God," these things are not going to change — so let's focus on what we can and must change.

It is no different in the public sector. Los Angeles Police Chief Willie Williams, formerly Police Chief in Philadelphia, is an advocate for "local policing," establishing storefront offices to serve local "markets." The needs of affluent neighborhoods, retail strip malls, industrial areas, and government housing are very different. The crimes are different, the criminals are different, and the resources required for security are different. By creating this local connection, they can establish relationships, insights, and information sources that greatly improve the effectiveness and efficiency of police work. Police officers are expected to live in the neighborhood and serve the neighborhood in order to truly understand and respond to its unique needs. It eliminates a lot of the "them vs. us" attitude that can so undermine local police work.

If you have the only product or service in town, and if it is in demand, you can force the market to conform to you. In mature industries, where customers have a lot of choices, we must serve unique needs. That means figuring it out one market at a time. Merril Stevenson, reporting for *The Economist*, described most distribution businesses when he wrote:

> Retail banking is really a market-by-market, streetcorner-by-streetcorner business. It is hard for the banks to formulate the kind of all-purpose winning strategy dear to the heart of every American manager.[8]

Initiatives on quality and customer focus often fail to provide ways to analyze and respond to unique local market needs. The result is rigid, unresponsive sales-and-service units locked into products and delivery routines that underperform in the local market. Even in emerging markets, a sure way to welcome competitors is to be unresponsive to local needs. The skills and focus of the local manager and his team are the single most important ingredient in winning or losing this local battle.

REASON 2: EFFICIENT CUSTOMER TARGETING

SINCE CUSTOMERS HAVE DIFFERENT NEEDS, we need an effective way of responding to those needs. This is best done locally. The Soviet

Union has given us a compelling 75-year study of the inefficiency of centralized planning. Free markets allocate resources more effectively (but not perfectly or without pain) than controlled markets. Free markets are local markets. The delivery of business products and services is no different in that respect than government products and services. I am often amazed by how many "free market" business executives and managers are running "central planning" units in their companies: Capitalist talk, but a socialist walk.

It makes sense that if needs are locally unique, people in the head office — often hundreds or thousands of miles, and perhaps states or countries, away — are *not* in the best position to dictate decisions regarding hours, staff, product mix, and service delivery. Different local markets require different solutions. Hispanic neighborhoods buy a different mix of grocery products, and many prefer dealing with Spanish-speaking check-out clerks. Young two-income families are likely to put a premium on quick, efficient service. Senior citizens may enjoy the social interaction of shopping for products or services; in banks they tend to "visit their money" often.

Product campaigns from the head office are often *not* the best use of resources for these local trade areas. Individual Retirement Account (IRA) campaigns (RSPs in Canada) in predominantly senior-citizen or college-student markets are not likely to be the most productive use of resources for maximizing profit or winning the priority markets, nor standard food product campaigns in ethnic consumer markets.

The battle cry that opens this chapter, passed along by Theodore Levitt in his book *The Marketing Imagination*, succinctly captures the spirit of the new competition. "Think Global" invites us to exploit the economies of scale for things that are best done in a centralized, consolidated mode (centralized processing, 1-800 customer information, image advertising). "Act Local" means we must focus sales, service, and market efforts in the most targeted way possible to win the streetcorner-by-streetcorner battle. Some of these key targeting decisions are much less obvious than age or ethnicity.

In a comment for *American Banker*, Kent Pelz said that in micromarketing the promotional decisions are shifting from the corporate staff to the individual branches, where more is known about customers and prospects, such as where they live and what they buy:

> Looking at the cost per thousand to reach consumers, macromarketing appears to have the edge. (A print campaign costs less than $15 per thousand.) Micromarketing may rely more on highly targeted direct mail, which can cost up to $750 per thousand or more. But it is important to note that there is much less wasted circulation with micromarketing than with macromedia distribution because the latter often delivers a high percentage of untargeted consumers. So localized marketing actually costs less, which, in these days of reduced marketing budgets, is especially appealing.[9]

Researchers of a recent University of Chicago Graduate School of Business study, which focused on whether supermarkets should adopt "everyday low prices," gave the following advice on marketing:

> Many grocers are misspending their marketing dollars by spreading them equally across an entire chain. [Instead,] supermarket operators should be allocating different amounts according to consumer needs and characteristics of a store's "micro-market." In some of those markets, the emphasis should be on price promotions. . . . In others, customers may be more interested in the quality of produce and meats, the variety of goods and other shopping amenities. Too often, the main reason retailers adopt certain prices is to match their competition. They ought to pay more attention to the people coming into their stores.[10]

The same concept of efficiency applies elsewhere. We see many examples where the centralized initiative is in direct conflict with the local strategy. Our consultants worked recently with five small business center managers in a bank with more than 200 business centers. As we finished analyzing market potential and targeting strategies and tactics for their trade areas, one of the managers made the following observation:

It is really refreshing to analyze our local situation before prescribing the solution. You know, our usual approach around here is to have a major initiative from head office (for example, sales training) to get everyone out selling and bringing in new customers. If we had employed the usual approach to these five centers, I can tell you what would have happened. The Smithville and Hampton centers have relatively low market share and they need to gain additional customers. They would have thought of sales training as part of a game plan to get new customers as a good idea. They have relatively new account managers who have received little training. Good idea for them.

The Johnson Center and my center, the Oak Center, have over 35 percent market share. We have more customers than we can service and Jim [the Johnson Center manager] and I are worried that our competitors will pick off some of our best clients because we are drowning in the volume coming at us. We have very experienced teams and they have all been to sales training. Some have been three times. The last thing we need to do is go after more customers. We can't handle the ones we have now. In fact, what we need is some training on how to streamline service delivery to our low-end customers or get more revenue from them. We also need to focus on retention and growth of our best customers.

Bill has the fifth center, Valley Center, that is still fighting some significant credit problems, a struggle in which his staff is totally involved. With Valley Manufacturing moving out of his community, a number of his small business clients are going to be affected. Sales training at this time would be the wrong focus. He is still trying to circle the wagons to minimize credit risk.

Why are people surprised that when head office rolls out a "let's go get more customers" campaign, it doesn't get support? Two out of five, or 40 percent, is not a great hit ratio. The good news is that some will simply blow it off. The others will bust a gut while every step of the way they know it is a dumb decision. It doesn't fit the marketplace nor the customers. The staff will become cynical and they'll come in last in the campaign.

Resources (staff, time, energy, customers, prospects) are too scarce to misallocate as though one size fit all. Efficiency comes from providing the right resources to the right markets at the right time and cost.

More and more businesses are adapting the strategy of acting local. Blockbuster Entertainment Corporation and IBM recently announced a joint venture to market a technology with which local retailers can make compact disks on demand, even mixing and matching songs from different albums.[11] *The Wall Street Journal* reports that a key part of Sears's new $4 billion renovation will include more of a local-market focus; the company plans to tailor the product mix in each store to the ethnic makeup of the community. It notes that other retailers, such as JCPenney and Kmart, have already made similar moves.[12]

When we think of targeting customers, the objective is not reaching the largest group nor getting the lowest cost per thousand. The question is, Which approach will yield the highest return or the most profit? A campaign that brings in 20 customers who contribute $1,000 each to our bottom line is better than one that brings 100 customers at $50 each. However, in some local markets, the $50 customer is our best bet. Effective targeting is not a volume or cost game; it is a productivity game based on profit contribution.

REASON 3: STAFF COMMITMENT

MARKET NEEDS ARE DIFFERENT, and efficient allocation of resources means targeting resources to those needs; over- or underdelivery creates inefficiency. This is the strategy behind acting local. We must remember, however, that the execution of strategy relies mainly on people. Peter Drucker says that in preparing a plan, the most important thing to consider is your scarcest resources.[13] I would submit that the most critical, scarcest resource for winning the local market is skilled, committed, focused staff and front-line managers.

The third reason that acting local is so important is that it is the best way to enhance the energy and accountability of local staff. To understand why this is so critical, think of the many acquisitions and consolidations over the past 10 to 20 years. As large companies gobbled up smaller ones, there was a diminution of local autonomy. Local owners and executives, who used to have their own boards, management committees, cars, country clubs, approval authority and raw power, were made store, branch, and regional managers. This was done to cut costs, which was very important, but for sales-and-service people the local perspective had some distinct advantages. It delivered local, close-to-the-marketplace decisions and actions. People felt good about their autonomy to do what was right for the customer; staff did not have far to go to get a decision. As customers, managers, and front-line staff watched autonomy and authority recede into the distance, many decisions no longer seemed to fit the local market. Customers were quite frequently upset by changes in procedures, credit requirements, and unfamiliar management.

Somewhere along the way a number of managers and front-line staff abdicated. One manager recently described it this way:

> We don't run anything around here anymore. It all comes from head office, they are making all of the decisions. Yet when it doesn't work, they come back and ask us why. Well, my opinion is that we are doing a number of things that just don't fit this market. I'll do what I am told but it is not my fault — I am just carrying out orders and keeping my nose clean. I have figured out that they don't want my ideas so I've stopped giving them. But, I'll tell you what — we used to beat the socks off that outfit across the street, and now they are giving us a real run for our money. And there is not a single person here that feels good about it.

The term that describes this attitude is *malicious obedience*. It is doing what you are told, rather than what is right for the customer, the staff, and the company. This level of abdication is a sure-fire formula for failure. It is a key reason why over 60 percent of the branch, store, and center managers we poll identify local independent stores, banks, airlines, and other local competitors as their single greatest competitive worry. It is interesting that while executives in the boardroom are most concerned about competitors with large distribution systems, managers in local markets are often most worried about local independents.

What does this really mean? It means that if we are to have inspired, energized, and accountable people for this competitive war we are in, then the larger we get, the smaller we must act. To a large extent the battle for the local marketplace is a battle for the hearts and souls of our people. We must create a work environment where their input, autonomy, and accountability create rather than dissipate energy.

Acting local means asking their opinions. They have many of the best answers, because they are closest to the customer. It means putting them back in charge of their markets and in control of their jobs. It means having them analyze the market potential, participate in planning, come up with the implementation actions — yes, tellers, service representatives, clerks, salespeople — because we can't win the battle without them. It also means making them accountable for the results.

Too often empowerment is described without including a critical component: accountability. My favorite cartoon shows a crowded organization chart with every box, from the front line to the CEO, containing the title "Victim." We have whole industries staffed by victims. The opposite of "victim" is "accountable." Empowerment is not a free ride; it is making choices and living with the consequences. Odds for success rise greatly when we educate, train, and provide tools for winning. In an empowered environment, more enabling occurs, more excuses are removed, and results are made more tangible.

There is no surer way to create an uninspired, uncommitted local sales and service team than to impose decisions and actions that are unresponsive to local market needs. When empowerment and accountability are absent, the monkey moves directly back to the boss. The energy, commitment, and focus of people are too critical to overall market success to let that happen.

THE POWER OF ACTING LOCAL

WHY ACT LOCAL? The varied needs of customers necessitate it. If we are going to be customer driven, we must be locally focused. It is a more efficient means of targeting local customers. If we are going to be productive, we must be oriented to the local market. Finally, it makes for the best use of our most critical resource — our people. If we want to be the best team, we must act local.

Again, acting local does not mean getting rid of "Central." Charles Handy, in *Harvard Business Review*, describes it quite well:

> The concept of federalism is particularly appropriate since it offers a well-recognized way to deal with paradoxes of power and control: the need to make things big by keeping them small; to encourage autonomy but within bounds, to combine variety and shared purpose, individuality and partnership, local and global, tribal region and nation state. . . .

> Neither, however, is federalism just a classy word for restructuring. The thinking behind it, the belief, for instance, that autonomy releases energy; that people have the right to do things in their own way as long as it is in the common interest; that people need to be well-informed, well-intentioned, and well-educated to interpret that common interest; that individuals prefer being led to being managed: these principles reach into the guts of the organization or, more correctly, into its soul — the way it goes about its business day by day. Federalism properly understood is not so much a political structure or system as it is a way of life.[14]

In acting local we are seeking the right balance. In most companies, balance means pushing more autonomy and accountability lower.

Acting local, quite simply, is a more productive model. For breakout performers, it provides a sustainable competitive advantage that makes it more customer driven, more targeted in application of resources, and a more effective approach for leading local staff and teams. Yet we all know that empowered, accountable local teams don't occur by accident. We will talk about development of the local, empowered team in part IV.

8

Segmenting Your Market

Knowing Where to Tap

66 There is an old story of a boilermaker who was hired to fix a huge steamship boiler system that was not working well. . . .

... After listening to the engineer's description of the problems and asking a few questions, he went to the boiler room. He looked at the maze of twisting pipes, listened to the thump of the boiler and the hiss of escaping steam for a few minutes, and felt some pipes with his hands. Then he hummed softly to himself, reached into his overalls and took out a small hammer, and tapped a bright red valve, once. Immediately the entire system began working perfectly, and the boilermaker went home. When the steamship owner received a bill for $1,000, he complained that the boilermaker had only been in the engine room for 15 minutes, and requested an itemized bill. This is what the boilermaker sent him:

For tapping with hammer:	$	.50
For knowing where to tap:		999.50
Total	$	1,000.00 [1]

*T*HE SECOND PRINCIPLE FOR BREAKOUT PERFORMANCE is segmentation. Before we get too deeply into segmentation as an organizational principle or strategy, it is important to understand where it comes from: customers. Think of the choices you make regarding where you get your haircut, buy groceries, get your car repaired, or have your clothes cleaned. Why do you choose certain vendors? Why do you rule out others? Convenience, price, quality, hours, flexibility: we all have reasons. As customers we segment constantly when we make buying decisions that get our needs met.

It is helpful to recognize the segmentation that has occurred across an entire industry or in a local market. In the life insurance industry, for example, Metropolitan Life's average policy size in 1992 was $91,690, compared with $206,485 at Equitable and $246,185 at Connecticut General Life. This difference, whatever the cause, reflects segmentation: different market segments are being tapped.[2]

WHO'S SEGMENTING WHOM?

SEGMENTATION AS A SMALL BUSINESS OR CORPORATE STRATEGY is simply a way of dealing with customer segmentation behavior. Segmentation is a principle that helps us become the store or airline or bank of choice for customers who value what we are (or could be) good at. Our segmentation strategies should be designed to make us more customer- and market-focused.

Willie Sutton, the famous bank robber, figured it out earlier than most. His legendary response to the question of why he robbed banks — "Because that's where the money is" — captures succinctly the essence of segmentation. We can just imagine him on the cover of *Fortune* with excerpts from his book (*Things Willie Sutton Might Have Said*?) updated into today's Corporate-speak:

> Well, you know, early on we looked at the market and we considered hardware stores, wealthy homeowners, trains, and a number of other possibilities, but I just kept coming back to banks as the segment that provided the greatest opportunity. Sure enough, the market research confirmed what we suspected, that there were thousands of banks and because of regulation they were pretty homogeneous. I mean, they all have a vault and a lobby and hours are fairly standard.
>
> When we inventoried our skills and experience, it was obvious that we matched up well with the market. We did not have the capital or experience to try to be all things to all people. We could not be a market leader in banks *and* trains. They are very different markets, plus the potential is much greater in banks. I kind of come from the Jack Welch school at GE — if you can't be first, second, or third in a market, then get out.

Yes, Willie knew to segment the market. He is not alone. Many companies are becoming experts in segmenting their markets:

> Diet Pepsi started this week on its mission to deliver one million cases of Diet Pepsi or Caffeine Free Diet Pepsi to the doorsteps of Diet Coke drinkers across the nation.... The soft-drink brand has dubbed April National "Uh Huh!" month (to tie in with its current musical ad campaign) and

has teamed with United Parcel Service, which will handle the deliveries. In addition to the soft drink, each package also contains a pop-up message from singer Ray Charles and a consumer survey. Consumers targeted for the blitz allegedly drink about twelve servings of Diet Coke per week.[3]

Consumers who drink about 12 servings of Diet Coke per week — *that* is getting serious about target groups within a segment.

LEARN TO THINK LIKE YOUR MARKET

EFFECTIVE SALES-AND-SERVICE DISTRIBUTION SYSTEMS must be very proactive in the local trade area in assessing the criteria that customers and prospects use to segment their product and service providers. In essence, we must learn to think like our local market. To optimize our return we may have to think like two or three separate groups. As we assess the criteria these customer groups use to meet their needs, we must consider how to position, tailor, and apply our products and services to appeal to these criteria. We must consider how to bring value — relevant value — to the market. And we must know how to do it within the range of our capabilities. We must explore how to attract profitable customers who value what we are good at. Over and again, it seems that breakout performers do this better than their peers.

The early wave of segmentation has focused more on product segmentation than on sales-and-service segmentation. Increasingly, however, sales-and-service staff must make the key decisions about how to segment sales and service to win local market groups.

There are three primary reasons why segmentation gives us a better return on our resources and customers better alternatives for meeting their needs.

REASON 1: WINNING TARGET GROUPS

WE ARE BETTER AT SELLING AND SERVICING certain customers, and we make more profit on some than on others. To optimize the local trade area, we must profitably win these target groups. When we get serious about winning these target groups, market segmentation leads to *differentiation* — the perception by target customer groups that we are a significantly better choice to meet their needs..

Henry Ford quickly learned that "any color you want, so long as it is black" was not competitive, because other manufacturers gave customers better choices. We have only to visit the soft-drink section of a grocery store to see how customer tastes vary. In the cola category, there used to be two primary choices — regular and low-cal. Now there are cherry, caffeine-free, sugar-free, caffeine-and-sugar-free, and crystal clear colas. Failure to provide these choices results in loss of market share.

The marketplace has been brutal to companies like Sears, IBM, and General Motors that have high cost but low differentiation. Twenty years ago, General Motors led the industry in providing different kinds of cars (Chevrolet, Buick, Cadillac) for different customer needs. However, in an effort to cut costs, GM began producing a range of models that sold at different prices but looked alike. At the same time, Mercedes, BMW, Volkswagen, Toyota and Honda began marketing models that broadened the range of upper- and lower-end choices. Later they expanded into GM's prime midrange markets. In response, GM's share dropped significantly.

Increasing competition from niche players is forcing larger service providers to be more specific in defining target groups. Recently our company was working with a local branch that wanted to attract more business from a generalized target group of professionals — lawyers, doctors, and accountants. When our local market analysis showed that the buying motives and potential profits were different for each profession, the bank decided to tailor strategies and tactics for each — to provide "profession-specific" differentiation.

A recent *Newsweek* article by David Ansen and Charles Fleming describes how segmentation is affecting the movie industry:

> The glory of the Hollywood studio system has always been its ability to turn out mass entertainment that could appeal to the entire spectrum of the audience — and win Oscars and critical acclaim. Think of "It Happened One Night" or "The French Connection" or "One Flew Over the Cuckoo's Nest" — or last

year's winner, "The Silence of the Lambs." Now even the biggest hits, like "Batman Returns," alienate half the audience or simply exclude adults, like "Home Alone 2." Hollywood can count on its prime ticket-buying public — teenage boys — to line up for the parade of "Lethal Weapons," "Die Hards," and Steven Seagal movies, but it has driven away millions of potential viewers in the process. (Ticket sales have dropped from 1.2 billion in 1983 to 950 million in 1992, and the largest drop has been for adult ticket buyers.) Since the studios have decided that women matter less than men in dollars and cents, it always catches them by surprise when a small "woman's film" like "Fried Green Tomatoes" turns into a runaway hit. You have to wonder if the boys in the Hollywood boardrooms, who seem to get younger and younger by the year, know that mass culture doesn't just mean kiddie culture.[4]

There are clearly consequences for being too broad or too narrow in targeting certain segments or groups.

It's a Matter of Giving Customers a Better Choice

Segmentation leads to differentiation — better choices for the customer. One of our company's largest banking clients has divided its small business market into two segments. It gave its small business customers two options, saying, in effect, "If what you value is the lowest possible rates and fees, choose our 'no frills' option. You will not be assigned an account manager, but when you need service, you can call in and talk with the first available banker. However, if what you value is an assigned account manager, we will provide a relationship banker who will call and visit you several times a year to analyze your business and personal financial needs and add value to your decisions. For this package, you will pay a monthly fee."

Regardless of whether this degree of segmentation is appropriate for all, there is no denying that it gives customers additional choices. It is important to note that the key is not necessarily providing more choices, because there are limits to how broad we can be; rather, it is providing the *right choices* to the *right markets*.

The current popularity of discount, self-help retailers is a reflection of the low value added by traditional sales clerks. The salesperson has traditionally filled orders, but with today's computers, automation, and electronic data interchange (EDI), there are faster, less costly, and more accurate ways. As a result, customers can choose to unbundle the cost of a salesperson from the cost of the purchase.

The Yardstick of the '90s: Value

There is a growing consensus among organizational strategists that either end of the value-added/low-cost spectrum is better than the middle — that customer buying motives now cluster at one end or the other. Positioning as lowest in cost or highest in quality — "branding" — seems to generate more pull than being in the middle. Keith Von Seggern, Director of Training at Firstar Bank Corporation, uses the Wal-Mart, Sears, Nordstrom continuum to help managers assess their positioning (fig. 8.1).

Branding based solely on advertising clout is also losing strength. For years, advertised "name" brands competed well against generic products, but in the value-conscious '90s, that is changing. For example, Oller and Associates, a unit of Information Resources, Inc., reports that while August–October sales of all cough and cold remedies in supermarkets and drugstores skidded 9 percent, sales of private-label cold and cough remedies jumped 9 percent during

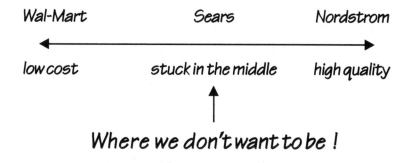

Figure 8.1. Low-Cost/High-Quality Spectrum

the same period.[5] In Canada, private labels such as President's Choice and Master's Choice now control almost 20 percent of the soft drink market, up from only 5 percent before the recession.[6] More than ever before, customers use the yardstick of value to evaluate the claims of familiar brands.

In a September 1992 Roper poll (published in *Fortune*) on the most important reasons for buying a brand, consumers chose price over quality by 17 percentage points.[7] In a similar poll in 1985, quality edged out price by two points. The percentage of consumers who say some brands are worth a premium price fell from 45 percent in 1988 to 37 percent in 1992. The study shows that Americans' definition of value has switched from "best in class" to "best in budget range."

Is this just a short-term phenomenon? In the same *Fortune* article, Grey Advertising research reported 72 percent of respondents saying they would never return to their old spending ways.[8]

Giving Customers What They Want

We must keep our attention focused on the single most important reason to segment: to be more customer driven, to give target customers more precisely what they want. The past few years' service quality efforts have largely assumed that all customers want and need the same things. Rather than focusing on the needs of target groups and designing service features that differentiate, we have given them what was easy for us to deliver or what we wanted all of them to have. The same has been true for sales efforts; concerned with volume, we have paid little attention to the customer mix needed to increase the value of a local franchise.

We don't have to look far to see differentiated service solutions that have evolved to meet the needs of customer groups: drive-through for fast food, purchase by phone or mail in direct-order retailing, convenience stores for the grocery business, independent car leasing specialists who eliminate the need to negotiate with automobile dealers, phone or video express checkout in hotels, home sales and delivery of groceries, self-service gasoline, and in-home sales of financial service products. None of these service delivery solutions is the best answer for all customers — but each is a best answer for one or more groups of customers. For them, differentiated service solutions increase value.

Treacy and Wiersema's *Harvard Business Review* article provides a good example:

> Kraft then determined for its major accounts which shopper groups frequented each of their stores. A Kraft sales team even persuaded one chain to create a drive-through window in stores where planners and dine-outs — people who plan their shopping trips and dine out often — were a large segment, making it more convenient for them to pick up staples between big shopping trips.[9]

Segmenting the market means providing differentiation for target groups. It is the accountability of local sales and service to identify the best targets that fit within the corporate strategy, and to deliver differentiation that will profitably win those targets.

REASON 2: ALLOCATING SCARCE RESOURCES

IF WE HAD UNLIMITED TIME, people, and capital, then we could dominate the entire marketplace — but we don't. IBM, Sears, and General Motors came close; and for a while, the airlines and banks were regulated, and thus insulated from competition. Today resources are scarce; in the few cases where they are plentiful, they will become scarce if not invested wisely.

Segmentation does two things to improve our use of these resources: it builds on our strengths, putting more resources into customer segments where our margins and profits are high, helping us retain and expand those segments; and it lowers the cost or increases the price in segments where we are losing money or have low margins. Beyond this, it makes us aware that, given our strengths and limitations, we are not always the best choice for some customers.

Segmentation is our primary tool for managing the opportunities and risks of a local market. This is true in all industries. For example, Budget Rent-a-Car reports that about 5 percent of its New York renters, mostly people who are not employees of big companies and who are not traveling by airplane, cause half of Budget's accidents that end in damage suits.[10] The challenge is not so much to keep from damaging cars as to avoid liability suits. In eight states, including New York, the car rental company is liable if the renter injures another driver or pedestrian. Budget president and CEO William N. Plamonder sums up the importance of understanding the opportunities and risks of certain market segments:

> The days of going out and fighting for market share without regard for profitability are over.[11]

The November 17, 1992 *Wall Street Journal* described what advertising agencies are doing to resegment their market:

> More ad agencies are walking away from low-margin accounts rather than struggle to stick by them. In the current protracted recession, advertisers have become steadily chintzier, and many on Madison Avenue stood by helplessly as the standard 15 percent agency commission on billings fell to a range of 10 percent to 12 percent. Now, it seems, ad shops are saying enough is enough.[12]

Ken Graham, editor of Financial Marketing Research Report for *Journal of Retail Banking*, sums it up:

> Every dollar spent in retaining unprofitable customers is more than a dollar wasted.[13]

The Risk of Being All Things to All People

What does it all mean? It means we must be clearer than ever before on whom we wish to attract and keep. We must wish it enough that we act on and invest in that segment. We cannot be all things to all people. In its World Class Retail Bank Performance Report, the Council on Financial Competition summarized the perils of traditional thinking:

> Building undifferentiated mass market share may actually dilute retail bank profitability, rather than grow it; winners

and losers in retail banking through the '90s will be decided by ability to grow share of retail segments providing the bulk of profitability.[14]

As we gain clarity on our strengths and weaknesses and local market potential, we must develop an enhanced ability to target. This means two things: first, we must target *whom* we will serve — not to ignore or exclude customers outside the target market, but to choose customers on whom we will focus additional resources. And second, we must redesign local service delivery to provide differentiation — valued differentiation — to the target group.

Matthew S. Olson and Kevin T. Murray of the Council for Financial Competition summed it up in the *American Banker*:

> We have found that top performers are either becoming market leaders in target markets, or else withdrawing. They are shaping market share strategies around well-defined demographic and geographic segments, as opposed to the mass market strategies of competitors.[15]

There are breakthrough opportunities for companies that find profitable but underserved target markets. Much of Wal-Mart's early success came from a targeting breakthrough. Conventional wisdom at that time among Kmart and other discounters was that it did not make sense to go to towns smaller than 50,000 people. Wal-Mart found it could make money in towns of 5,000 or fewer. Its targeting strategy was simple: Go where they ain't. It works even better when your target niche is big enough for one local discount store but not two — particularly if you are the first to get there.

Better Sales and Service for Some, Lower Cost for Others

Once we have answered the "who" part of the segmentation question, we must deal with the "how." We must design and engineer service levels that create value for our chosen segment(s) of customers and prospects. We must create value for them in a way that also creates value for the corporation — that is, profitably. We are not doing our customers any favors if, in the long run, we lose money.

Going out of business is not a recognized service enhancement strategy for most customers. Some high-cost, low-value service initiatives miss this point.

Large department stores face this difficult challenge: they need to lower cost to reduce the discounters' price advantage, yet superior service is their strongest potential advantage. This challenge is especially difficult because, in many cases, the discounters serve their customers well. A *Wall Street Journal* article describes the service approach of R.H. Macy & Company:

> [Macy's] is strategically detailing salespeople to so-called "relationship" departments, such as luggage and jewelry, where shoppers need extra assistance. Others — such as hosiery — are deemed "convenience" departments, and shoppers are on their own.[16]

The article goes on to describe a similar segmentation strategy in the Bloomingdale's division of Federated Department Stores:

> Clerks have offered Godiva chocolates and sent out thank-you notes to preferred shoppers, who are also invited to private shopping nights where the store bestows such "Gifts of Service" as free alterations and free local delivery of furniture.[17]

This level of differentiated service provides some real cultural challenges. It is difficult to argue for less service for some market segments, particularly in a culture like Macy's, Bloomingdale's, or Nordstrom's that prides itself on premier service for all. Yet if customers do not value it enough to pay for it, something must change.

As we have shown, setting dual objectives of better service and lower cost leads directly to segmentation: lower cost for some segments and better service for others. Unless we segment, we will be neither the least expensive nor the best. We'll be stuck in the middle — undifferentiated. We can currently see in the mutual fund business how these strategies evolve.

> With $164 billion in assets under management, Fidelity is the unsurpassed leader in the mutual fund industry. But the full-service financial firm faces brutal competition on many

fronts. The industry's furious growth during the 1980s may be slowing; investors' choices are exploding. Investors today can choose among 3,423 mutual funds — five times more than a decade ago.

Vanguard is certainly one of Fidelity's most tenacious competitors. It is focused on one target: selling mutual funds directly to investors. To do that, [Vanguard CEO John C.] Bogle has successfully positioned Vanguard as a provider of low-fee funds and the company is expected to benefit from the 1990s frugality fad.

Fidelity, in contrast, has set the broad goal of being all things to all investors — broker, investment adviser, and money manager. As such, it competes with an array of firms, from discount broker Charles Schwab & Co. to Wall Street giant Merrill Lynch.[18]

This is the classic battle between the large, broad, older firm and the smaller, narrower, emerging firm, a battle that occurs over and over: IBM vs. Compaq, Compaq vs. Dell, American Airlines vs. Southwest, General Motors vs. Nissan or Honda, Sears vs. Wal-Mart, numerous department stores vs. The Gap. There are many reasons for success or failure in these battles. Many people consider being the lowest-cost provider as the key principle — and during a recession, that is a successful segmentation strategy. But the larger principle is targeting and serving your market better than anyone else. Just as the '80s brought designer labels and image and the early '90s brought low cost and frugality, the next era will call for new segments, new targets. It will not always be possible to hit the hot cycles, but lasting success can be achieved by targeting and serving your chosen markets better than anyone else.

We have only so many dollars to spend. As Bum Phillips, former head football coach of the Houston Oilers, once said about head coach Don Shula of the Miami Dolphins, "He can take *his* and beat *yours* or he can take *yours* and beat *his*."[19] As local market managers, that is what we must do. We must take the available resources and obtain the best return possible in our local market. We must make our system more productive than theirs. If we can get a greater return from our dollars than the competition, then we can optimize and profitably win the local market.

REASON 3: INCREASING VALUE TO CUSTOMERS

IN TOO MANY INDUSTRIES, WE HAVE FAILED TO APPLY the acid test of value: being the best choice for a target group. To revisit Stanley Marcus: Is the product or service good enough that our customers are willing to pay us a profit for it?[20] One of the primary challenges of sales and service is to ensure this accountability, target group by target group. Too often, because of our sheer size and volume, we lose track of this fundamental truth. While we lose money on one group of customers, we overcharge others to get our average cost, revenue, and profits in line. The niche player goes after the overcharged high-profit group, giving them a better deal but still bringing in a nice profit.

Overcharged customers who are subsidizing loss leaders will not be loyal indefinitely. As this high-profit customer segment defects, overall revenue declines faster than cost. The enterprise is left with too high a proportion of unprofitable customers and a cost structure designed for the previous customer mix, not the current mix. The enterprise goes into a nose dive because it is difficult to cut costs fast enough to offset revenue defection from the high-profit segment.

We must assess our value delivery market by market and target group by target group. As an executive of a large banking division said:

> Figures lie and liars figure. But our numbers show that we just had the best quarter in two years. Yet when I look under the numbers, our customer profitability system indicates that we are losing more than $70 annually on over 40 percent of our customers. It is hard for me to get truly excited about a great quarter when I analyze this underlying weakness.

We should all examine success so rigorously. His organization is suffering market share erosion in its most profitable market segment. Even though his company is profitable today due to interest rate spreads, he knows it is his job to deal with the value issue. Competitors can potentially win this value battle, and he sees the early warning signs. Yes, profits are up and volume is stable, but as head of sales and service, he knows his A-market segmentation solution is losing ground. He and his general manager are planning to reengineer sales and service for this high-value segment because they know that current success is based on conditions and actions taken several months ago. They are acting now to create future success.

Does this mean that large, old, broad market leaders are doomed? It does, if they continue to act like large, old, broad companies. But if they can act local and small, empower people, and segment their markets one at a time, they can survive and prosper.

Fortune magazine asked a similar question about Microsoft, Bill Gates's huge software corporation: Can they compete against a horde of specialized niche players?

> Microsoft is unique in trying to compete in virtually every niche — and it never, never surrenders. "Like the Japanese, they get it wrong several times before they get it right," says Richard Shaffer, editor of *ComputerLetter*.[21]

What are the critical elements for Microsoft? According to Jeff Raikes, head of U.S. sales at the company:

> Don't get complacent.... Be willing to take risks. Stay frugal.[22]

How do they view the market?

> Microsoft ranks No. 1 overall in software, but in most categories of applications it's No. 2, No. 3 or No. 4 — and obsessively focused on the market leader. When Jeff Raikes was in charge of Microsoft's word-processing software, Gates challenged him to learn everything about Pete Peterson, who ran the top competitor, WordPerfect. Raikes took Gates literally: he even memorized the names, ages and birthdays of Peterson's six children.... Microsoft is organized into small bands of people with a mission who can pound, pound, pound.[23]

Segmentation Provides Precision Needed for Breakout Performance

Can a large company remain a market leader? Yes, if it is market focused, acts small, and concentrates on the mission. However, points are not awarded unless we meet the ultimate goal. That is, we must use our targeting and our resource allocation to create value. It is hard to imagine quality, productivity, or customer focus succeeding as sustainable strategies without segmentation. Segmentation is the use of a precision instrument in place of a blunt instrument. To be breakout performers, we need precision in managing sales and service.

To summarize: Why do we segment? Because it is the best way to focus on target groups, and the best way to allocate scarce resources. The risk of not segmenting is that we may lose our profitable customers and overspend on our loss leaders.

Segmentation is a fact of the marketplace. We can either anticipate the market and chart our intentions, or we can take what is left. At the corporate level or at the local level, failure to segment will make us a magnet for the least profitable customers.

Many industries are extremely vulnerable to this risk — yet for the same industries, segmentation provides huge opportunities for productivity improvement. The next chapter outlines these opportunities and risks.

9

Getting Breakthrough Productivity

Creating Efficiencies in the Customer Factory

66 When it came to leaving the three of us boys to perform a shared task like cutting weeds, Papa's insight about the number of sons assigned the work and the level of productivity obtained was this: One boy is a boy; two boys is half a boy, and three boys is no boys at all. 99

— *My father, on his father*

173

*A*CT LOCAL. SEGMENT YOUR MARKETS. These are essential principles. They lead us to a third important principle: getting breakthrough productivity. Very simply, breakthrough productivity means our sales-and-service delivery system must cost less and/or produce more.

Why is productivity so important? If we are not highly productive in the design, engineering, and creation of profitable customer relationships, we have two alternatives. We can pass our productivity "overcharges" on to the customer in the form of pricing, using marketing as a means of convincing the customer of the value of the "brand." For years, the American Express card was perceived by both card members and business establishments (particularly restaurants) as image worth the price. Recently, however, their loss of market share indicates that when customers really considered value, the price was perceived to be too high.

Our other alternative is to keep prices competitive and sell at low margins or a loss. The major airlines seem to be trapped in this predicament. They are transporting large volumes of passengers from Point A to Point B at a price that is below their cost. When such historically successful carriers as American and Delta have protracted operating losses, you begin to look for basic structural problems in their industry that relate to productivity.

As we look for ways to achieve productivity breakthroughs, it is useful to note how much improvement is possible. Michael Hammer, the consultant usually credited with coining the term "reengineering," says:

> Most companies have a lot of people whose functions don't add any value to the product or service. They are the corporate glue that holds the real work together. When you design the real work better, you need a lot less glue.[1]

How much less glue? According to *The Wall Street Journal:*

> U.S. manufacturers employ virtually the same number of production workers as they did in 1946 — about 12 million — to produce roughly five times as many goods.[2]

The article goes on to say that a growing number of service companies are initiating reengineering programs to improve productivity. Much of that reengineering is in product creation and delivery, less has been done to reengineer sales and service in local markets. Our challenge is to make sales-and-service delivery five times as productive.

Now we come to the fundamental point. Too often we treat productivity problems as if they were simply cost problems. This is short-sighted; productivity is the relationship of revenue to cost. In the short run, we can always cut costs and achieve immediate productivity gains. We could fire all management, for example, and much of the service support organization that does not directly generate revenue, and thereby increase short-term productivity. Why? Because customer defection doesn't occur instantaneously. The process usually goes something like this:

1. Noticing service deterioration

2. Experiencing a problem

3. Complaining or silently expecting restoration

4. Considering alternatives

5. Deciding to defect

Not everyone goes through these exact steps or at the same speed, but the "currency" in the "customer loyalty bank" means that customer defection lags behind service deterioration. This is why many studies indicate that cost reduction initiatives neither increase productivity nor, in the long run, lower cost. They can disguise core productivity problems and delay dealing with the real causes. When our better customers start defecting, revenue and profits go down, time spent in customer recovery goes up, and as a result, a minor productivity problem can become a train wreck.

The acid test for cost reduction is productivity. After we reduce costs, does each remaining dollar of cost give us more sustainable revenue than before? Anything less than a yes means we are just shrinking the enterprise. But as service providers, we must go beyond this output/input definition of productivity. When we shift our view of productivity from how much we can produce per dollar (for example, number of widgets) to how much value we can create for the customer (sustainable or lifetime revenue and price), we move to a market perspective — productivity that matters.

Too Much Cost — or the Wrong Cost?

This is not to say that cost reduction is unimportant. It is crucial! But it must be strategic and sustainable, and at the end of the day it must boost productivity. Often our biggest problem is not too much cost, but wrong cost. For example, many companies learned in the '80s that opulent buildings, furnishings, and surroundings added little value for customers.

So how do we gain productivity? It comes down to value. *Acting local* lets us identify the real opportunity in a local market, and keeps us from wasting time and resources doing things that don't fit the market. *Segmentation* lets us target resources to provide the right sales and right service to the right customer groups at the right cost. To gain breakthrough productivity, to operate efficiently in the customer factory, we must combine these two principles with three market-driven approaches to doing business.

APPROACH 1: OWNING VERSUS RENTING CUSTOMERS

IN THE CUSTOMER FACTORY, "RENTING" — signing up new clients with no strategy for keeping them — is more expensive than "owning" customers. "Owning" means committing to a "customer lifetime," dealing with the customer's problems and needs, and providing services that are productive for the customer and profitable for the company.

Short-term relationships with customers are expensive, typically do not yield high returns, and reduce productivity. Replacing lost customers costs money — not only the lost revenue from the former customer, but the expense of signing up the new one. If we spend $5,000 to acquire a top commercial account, that cost is a good investment — if we keep the customer 10 or 15 years. According to the Council on Financial Competition, the customer's net present value — that is, expected profit for the expected customer tenure, expressed in today's dollars — is $188,000.[3] That's a good deal, if the customer stays that long. But if he or she leaves us ten months later, we lose money.

In the computer-leasing business, we see the same thing. It often takes one to three years to reach break-even on a deal to cover the cost of sales. A 5 percent increase in customer retention has the effect of lowering average cost per life insurance policy by 18 percent. The same improvement can increase profitability by 50 to 85 percent in banks and brokerage firms.[4] No wonder businesses are paying heed to customer retention.

The pressure for retention in insurance and other financial service businesses is particularly high because opening and closing accounts is very time-consuming and expensive. The same time spent cross-selling, serving, or attracting the right lifetime customers yields a better return. An analysis by Bain & Company shows how a retail bank deposit customer becomes more profitable over time (fig. 9.1).[5]

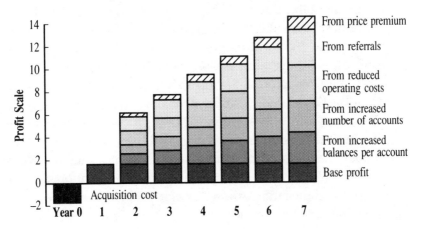

Adapted from Loyalty/Retention Practice, Bain & Company, Inc. ©Bain & Company, Inc.

Figure 9.1. Key Contributors to Overall Profitability

Although people hold different views on how and why profits from steady customers increase over time, there is no disagreement that productivity suffers as customer defection increases. Yet the front-line staff may be hardly aware of a silent but dramatic erosion of customers from their company, in an environment where goals and tracking are focused on product volume and not share of wallet or customer retention.

A Difference in "Share of Wallet" Opportunities

Few businesses disagree with the concept of owning customers, but few have set up the critical information systems, goals, practices, and skills needed to apply the concept. In 1989 a client with more than six million customers came to us with a problem. Their research showed that, although they were not losing customers, they were losing share of wallet from their upper-end customers — the top 15 percent. They were alarmed; much of their profit came from this group. They knew their profit plans, based on lowering costs and improving productivity, would be jeopardized by the loss of the large-ticket sales at the upper end. In fact, if they exchanged large-ticket sales for a larger number of smaller sales, their revenue would remain stable but servicing and processing costs would rise.

Like most businesses, they had no way to track this trend, either in aggregate or at the local market level. They had identified the problem only through market research. They had no goals for penetration or retention of the top 15 percent, no tracking mechanisms, no tactics to deal with the problem. Like most large retail distribution systems, they were tracking product revenue, number of complaints, customer satisfaction, and costs. Even though they could track these locally, regionally, and nationally, they could not track by market segments. Their management information systems obscured the single largest, most strategic problem they faced. Can you imagine running a factory without knowing how well or how many you are producing of product A vs. product B? Yet that is exactly how most large distribution systems are being run. We do not know whether we are gaining or losing A customers, or whether our overall amount of business with them is growing or shrinking. It's like running a factory in the dark, never knowing exactly what's coming off the assembly line.

The efficient and productive sales factory yields low customer defections. It takes raw material — target customers and prospects — and converts them into finished product — fully matured relationships, with a minimum of wasted effort or "scrap" (in the customer business, scrap becomes business for competitors). As cold and mechanical as this description sounds, productivity requires warm, focused, caring efforts, thousands per day, by people who are committed to serve.

Keep in mind that an efficient customer factory can also "own" C customers, not just A and B customers, even though most companies focus more on A customers. However, some of the most profitable local markets are composed predominantly of C customers. Why? Because local market managers figured out how to provide efficient, low-cost service to them and make a profit doing it.

Our firm recently worked with a distribution system that sells to small businesses in a metropolitan trade area. One of the salespeople had a customer base of mostly A customers. Everyone thought his overall profit contribution would be the highest, but when we conducted the analysis, we found that another salesperson in his office who had almost exclusively C customers brought in more profit because he was able to handle five times as many accounts (table 9.1).

Salesperson 1	Salesperson 2
30 A accounts	150 C accounts
× $2,000 profit each	× $500 profit each
= $60,000 profit	= $75,000 profit

Table 9.1. Profit Contribution Comparison

Although an exception to the rule, this example shows the beauty of optimizing the available potential. It also shows the fallacy of the excuse, "My market doesn't have high-profit customers." Effective market managers use productivity to optimize whatever is available to them — to profitably win the local market.

APPROACH 2: CHANGING THE NATURE OF THE WORK

SOMETIMES TOP EXECUTIVES SEE INDICATORS AND AVERAGES that make them think their costs are too high. Examples of benchmarks that might cause high-level heartburn include —

- Branch staff per 1,000 customers
- Passenger miles per employee
- Hotel rooms per employee
- Deposit dollars per FTE (full-time employee/equivalent)
- Personnel costs per dollar of revenue
- Revenue dollars per employee

Such benchmark comparisons may represent symptoms, indicating that something is wrong — but often tell us very little about the root cause. Treating the symptom may numb the pain, but the disease goes on. Peter Drucker, in an article for *The Wall Street Journal*, wrote:

> Cutting staffs to cut costs is putting the cart before the horse. The only way to bring costs down is to restructure the work. This will then result in reducing the number of people needed to do the job, and far more drastically than even the most radical staff cutbacks could possibly do. Indeed, a cost crunch should always be used as an opportunity to re-think and to re-design operations.[6]

Many businesses have experienced the short-term rewards of removing resources, only to find themselves struggling with customer service, employee morale, and customer defection problems six to eighteen months later. Having left themselves no alternative, they learn to restructure the work to some extent; necessity is the mother of invention. But few invent breakthroughs. Most lack the time, skill, empowerment, or innovation to reinvent their purpose.

Looking for Productivity Breakthroughs

How do we change the nature of the work? First, we must move beyond the fallacy of the average. If you have one foot in a pot of boiling water and another in a freezer of ice, "on average" you are comfortable. In the real world, you are in a lot of pain — and so are many of our customer factories.

As we have shown, even if our *average* cost is comparable to that of our competitors, we may be spending too much for some segments, causing us to lose margins; and we may be losing customers and profits by underdelivering to others. But if we reallocate the resources and restructure the work, we can achieve significant productivity breakthroughs (fig. 9.2).

Given a branch or store with:

5,000 customers

$400,000 in profit

$80 average profit/customer

If ...   20 percent of the customers = 80 percent of profits, and 80 percent of the customers = 20 percent of profits

If ...   80 percent of staff time is spent serving 80 percent of the customers who produce 20 percent of the profits

If ...   20 percent of staff time is spent serving 20 percent of the customers who produce 80 percent of the profits ($320,000)

If ...   We get the same level of contribution from the 80 percent of staff time that we are getting from the "high" 20 percent (4 × $320,000 = $1,280,000)

Then ...   The staff contribution could grow from $400,000 in profits to $1,600,000.

Figure 9.2. The Productivity Problem

Some productivity gains can be achieved by implementing across-the-board changes — for example, improvements in technology or work processes. Others, however, can be generated only by reallocating resources and restructuring the work to fit the local market. In some markets, resources must be redirected to retain and grow high-value customers whom we seldom see. In others, heavy solicitation of high-potential prospects is the key; in yet others, a predominance of C customers requires us to be a lean, mean customer-processing machine. The reengineering and reallocation of sales, service, and cost — a profound change in how we do business — must fit the market needs and potential.

Without a game plan for changing how we do the work, we may be unhappy with the random way that time and effort get allocated to target groups when we cut costs. Applying efficiency improvements indiscriminately may actually damage productivity, particularly if it runs off our best customers.

APPROACH 3: TARGETED COST REDUCTION

THE REASONS COMPANIES TACKLE THE CHALLENGES of cost reduction and productivity vary greatly — as do the understanding and sophistication of their approaches. In most companies, cost reduction is mandated as an aggregate goal or a required percentage. Someone decides that a 10 percent or 20 percent cut is needed. The magic number is administered like a dose of medicine, with two objectives:

1. Get to the goal.
2. Inflict the pain evenly.

By inflicting pain across the board, we hope to ensure buy-in: everyone gets hit, so it must be fair.

The following charts are provided to help companies assess their purpose and approach as they target cost reduction goals. Not all businesses go through all the levels, but most experience at least one or two.

Level 1: A Matter of Survival

In Level 1, cost is the only concern; little attention is given to how work or resources will be allocated (table 9.2). In a merger where duplication must be eliminated, or in a turnaround where survival is the goal, Level 1 cost reduction may be the only solution. Your company is on the tracks and the train is coming. There is little time for discussion or consensus. Chrysler, Bank of America, and the City of New York are a few of the organizations that have experienced Level 1 in the past two decades.

Such emergency cost reduction tells us what we must get rid of, but it provides little instruction on what we wish to become. Cutting costs across the company by 15 percent (Level 1) is very different from becoming the market leader by virtue of being the low-cost provider (Level 3). In Level 1, costs are usually cut both in production and in sales and service.

	Level 1	Level 2	Level 3	Level 4
Strategy:	Consolidation/ survival			
Goal:	Absolute cost reduction			
Solution:	Large cuts by a small executive team			
Market Focus:	None			
Leverage:	Quantity & speed of cost reduction			
Organization Focus:	Central — no time for consensus			

Table 9.2. Cost and Productivity Management, Level 1

	Level 1	Level 2	Level 3	Level 4
Strategy:	Consolidation/ survival	Competitiveness		
Goal:	Absolute cost reduction	Competitive costs		
Solution:	Large cuts by a small executive team	Tithing — every unit gives 10%		
Market Focus:	None	Parity with the competition		
Leverage:	Quantity & speed of cost reduction	Profit based on lower cost		
Organization Focus:	Central — no time for consensus	Departmental — share the pain		

Table 9.3. Cost and Productivity Management, Level 2

Level 2: "Go Out and Get It"

Level 2 is much like Level 1 (table 9.3). Managers are given a percentage goal; the main objective is to get the cost down and stay competitive, while spreading the pain evenly. But in Level 2 cuts, managers can choose or recommend where the cuts are made.

The problem with Level 2 is that it gives a mixed bag of results. Some of the cuts increase productivity a lot, some very little, and some hurt service delivery and drive away our best customers. Long-term results may be negligible or even negative. The costs of undoing the damage may surpass the savings.

There are many examples where companies eliminated employee training to reduce cost, only to find that slower customer handling, more complaints, new expenses for customer recovery (waived fees, giveaways), and customer defections cost the business ten, twenty, or a hundred times as much as the training had.

Level 3: Create Efficiencies by Right Sizing

In Level 3 we move from a defensive posture — "Are we too expensive?" — to an offensive posture: "We are going to be lowest cost" (table 9.4). To be "lowest cost," we must reengineer processes across functions to become more efficient and get rid of steps that add cost but no value. This objective is a step forward; it leads to real changes in the way work is done that can generate more revenue and more profits.

However, Level 3 falls short in two ways. One, its traditional approach to reengineering may ignore the local sales-and-service unit's need to optimize the potential in the trade area. How can we tailor local resources to be the provider of choice for the critical target groups needed to win that market? If we are inadequately resourced or focused in a rapidly growing market, the vacuum will quickly attract competitors with ample focus and resources.

A second problem occurs when allocation of resources and effort is based solely on volume. Many target staffing studies performed

	Level 1	Level 2	Level 3	Level 4
Strategy:	Consolidation/ survival	Competitiveness	Market share	
Goal:	Absolute cost reduction	Competitive costs	Low-cost leader	
Solution:	Large cuts by a small executive team	Tithing — every unit gives 10%	Reengineering central & local processes	
Market Focus:	None	Parity with the competition	Least cost in the market	
Leverage:	Quantity & speed of cost reduction	Profit based on lower cost	Revenue & profit based on least cost	
Organization Focus:	Central — no time for consensus	Departmental — share the pain	Cross-functional	

Table 9.4. Cost and Productivity Management, Level 3

by outside consulting firms fail to consider the makeup of the customer base or growth trends in the trade area when assessing staffing, work practices, and skill requirements. If we base staff only on the number of customers or transactions, we ignore the size and complexity of the transactions, and perhaps market potential, factors that significantly affect labor requirements and profit potential.

Level 4: Market-Driven Cost Reduction

In Level 4, the objective is *profitable* market dominance (table 9.5). Focusing on productivity and profit through revenue and cost management, this level is designed to provide value for multiple market segments: for high-value customers, differentiated service that fits their unique needs; for the C market, streamlined, efficient service at a cost and price that works for the customer and the business.

Market-driven cost reduction concentrates on productivity. It may cut overall expenses, but more significantly, it frequently

	Level 1	Level 2	Level 3	Level 4
Strategy:	Consolidation/ survival	Competitiveness	Market share	Profitable market dominance
Goal:	Absolute cost reduction	Competitive costs	Low-cost leader	Productivity & profit across market segments
Solution:	Large cuts by a small executive team	Tithing — every unit gives 10%	Reengineering central & local processes	Reengineering & reallocation based on market potential
Market Focus:	None	Parity with the competition	Least cost in the market	Best value for target markets
Leverage:	Quantity & speed of cost reduction	Profit based on lower cost	Revenue & profit based on least cost	Revenue & profit based on best customers & best costs
Organization Focus:	Central — no time for consensus	Departmental — share the pain	Cross-functional	Market focused — centrally, locally, cross-functionally

Table 9.5. Cost and Productivity Management, Level 4

reallocates costs, removing it from target groups that are loss leaders and reassigning it to target groups where the potential and, ultimately, the payoff are high.

Because sales and service usually focus so much of their attention on volume and customer satisfaction, they often abdicate their responsibilities for productivity. This has allowed "bean counters," less sensitive to markets but sometimes obsessed with profit and loss, to fill the void with short-term fixes. But if cost reduction is not to be simply a "going-out-of-business" strategy, we must get it market focused. Level 4 provides the model for dominating multiple markets based on central, local, and cross-functional market-driven productivity.

RETHINKING OUR BUSINESS

TO SERVE MULTIPLE MARKETS PRODUCTIVELY AND PROFITABLY, we must view our customers and our business differently; we must shift our attention from the random average customer to specific streams of customers with different profit contributions (fig. 9.3).

To reengineer the way we deliver sales and service, we must allocate costs to these customer and market streams according to their potential profitability. We know that customer mix is crucial, so we must understand revenue, cost, profit, and value for each stream in the mix.

Although we can develop guidelines corporately, they must be tailored to each local market because the makeup of each is different, the labor cost is different, and — even within market streams — customers are unique individuals. An executive who makes $150,000 a year in Manhattan may have little in common with a farmer making $150,000 in Stuttgart, Arkansas, in terms of needs, service preferences, relative ranking, and potential profit contribution.

Finally, when we evaluate the cost and productivity of our sales and service, we must ask a very tough question: How much of our revenue is being caused, or created, by the sales organization?

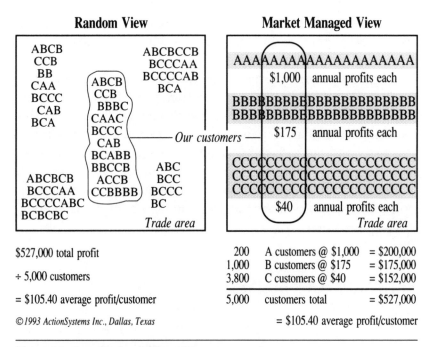

Figure 9.3. Same Market, Different Views

Just because revenue is going up or down does not mean that our distribution system is causing it, or that the delivery channel, employee skill sets, or service are maximizing value to the customer and the shareholder. IBM's distribution system was considered great until Compaq arrived — and Compaq's looked outstanding until Dell appeared. When revenue is up, the sales organization often takes the credit. It is like sending lettuce by rabbit — the outcome is easy to predict. I recently asked one company's head of sales what kind of year they were having. His response was insightful:

> Revenue is up over 10 percent; we are having a good year. I wish I felt better about it, though. I swear the growth would be there if we dissolved the sales organization. I am concerned that in this strong market we have an anemic contribution by sales. We are paying an awful lot in cost of sales. I am concerned we are not causing much of the growth. The question is: Is our sales organization profitable? Is it *causing* more than it is costing?

Gaining breakthrough productivity means changing the game by owning customers, particularly targeted customers. Everyone knows this, but most companies are stuck in an old product/volume paradigm that ignores the opportunities and hazards of customer streams.

Productivity requires moving beyond the battle cry of cost reduction and into the heavy lifting part of the job: changing the nature of the work, streamlining delivery to the C's, working more closely with the A's, and delivering value across all segments.

Finally, productivity means making choices not only about where costs will be eliminated but also where costs are reassigned. It requires looking at cost reduction as an investment strategy. It necessitates asking, What is our distribution system causing? Do I bank the cost savings or invest them in retaining, growing, and attracting target customers?

A BETTER BUSINESS THEORY

WE HAVE COME FULL CIRCLE in part III. Why do breakout performers do so well? Because they are doing things that less successful companies don't. To use Drucker's phrase, they have found and implemented a better business theory.[7]

This better business theory for sales and service rests on three important principles:

- Acting local, because that is the best way to meet customer needs and the most efficient and productive model for gaining valued contribution from our staff;

- Segmenting our market, because that is the best, most productive way to profitably win target groups by giving them the value they want; and

- Getting breakthrough productivity by owning customers, changing the nature of the work, and targeting cost to customer and market streams.

PART

IV

MARKET DRIVEN

*Making
the Change*

We have talked about the problems of the traditional approach to customer and market management. We have described the shortcomings and risks of a series of waves that fail to address the real problem — and in the process we presented a model that helps us manage the risk. We have defined three principles that guide our thinking in moving to local market management: acting local, segmenting the market, and achieving breakthrough productivity.

In part IV, we shift our focus to installing the solution. What must we change in order to implement these principles and put in place a fully functioning market-management strategy? How do we overcome the inertia of sales-and-service practices under an old business theory — practices that may have once propelled us to leadership in our industry, but which cannot deal adequately with the needs of today's customers, or the continuous improvement of hungry new competitors and reinvented old ones?

My colleagues and I have spent the past five years helping client businesses implement local market management. In the final chapters of this book, I will attempt to outline what we have learned about installing the change. We certainly don't know it all — and it is constantly evolving — but we have learned much that can be passed along and profitably used.

Not surprisingly, we have found that most companies underestimate the extent of the change required. Too often, they implement one aspect of the process — collecting better data, tiering customers, developing customer profitability models, requiring market plans — then sit back and await the good news. The result is, predictably, similar to what happened when businesses rode the sales and service waves: one problem cleaned up, two problems created.

This approach misses the point of local market management. Achieving competitive success in the '90s and beyond will take more than patching up the old system. It will demand a different way of looking at the delivery of sales and service — a new way that is in some respects an old way, that recalls the days when store owners, salespersons, and customers were friends and neighbors living on the same streets.

Installation of local market management requires big-time cultural change. It must engage every person from the top of the organization to the storefront.

In this final part of the book, we will begin by defining the context for cultural change and the steps to achieving it. We will outline the four key building blocks for installing market management; then we will define and describe the practices of a market manager. In the last two chapters, we will focus on obstacles, and on perhaps the highest hurdle of all — making the decision to act.

10

Transforming the Organization

It's Cultural Change, Stupid

66 Education is a bigger factor in productivity growth than increased capital, economies of scale or better allocation of resources. **99**[1]

— *David Kearns,*
Former CEO, Xerox Corporation

*I*N THE 1992 U.S. PRESIDENTIAL CAMPAIGN, the Clinton campaign staff erected a sign in their headquarters to keep them focused on the central issue they agreed held the key to winning the Presidential election: "It's the economy, stupid." This ever-present reminder kept everyone riveted on the central issue.

In the context of market management, "stupid" refers to me and to you on those occasions when we get distracted from the core issue. The central issue for local market management is not analysis or planning or customer profitability or tiering of customers. All of these are important components, but for lasting success, the central issue is cultural change.

Now it seems that there is always someone preaching cultural change to us. It gets a little old, doesn't it? But as true leaders, that is always our job. If marketplace needs did not change, if competition did not change, and if we were perfect, little management or leadership would be needed.

The corporate landscape is littered with companies and leaders who did not get it. Unfortunately, it is also littered with those who got it — who knew change was needed — but came up with the wrong strategy, or the right strategy poorly implemented. Michael Porter, of strategic planning fame at Harvard, has said that a B strategy with A implementation is better than A strategy with B implementation.[2]

The toughest part of implementation is getting the company to embrace the change. Organizational change is like an organ transplant: the surgery can be performed, but can we get the body to accept the new tissue?

It is easy for us to lament the difficulty of change. The bottom line is that change of any kind is not easy. As much as we might wish for an easier road to our destination, our energies are probably best directed at building a better map.

It is important to point out that the subject of cultural change is indeed complex. There are many good books available on the topic. Our purpose here is not to replow that ground, but rather to highlight key change issues that are paramount to installation of market management.

CULTURAL CHANGE AND ORGANIZATIONAL LEARNING

WHAT IS THE TRUE CHALLENGE in installing a market management culture? Yes, it is cultural change. But what is at the root of this challenge? Cultural change is best understood and treated in the context of learning. In his book *The Fifth Discipline*, Peter Senge says that highly successful organizations learn things that less successful organizations don't.[3] An organization that fails to learn how to respond to the ever-changing needs of the marketplace becomes culturally bankrupt before it becomes financially at risk. The strength of the cultural balance sheet — the assets and liabilities associated with the company's learning or skill sets — ultimately predicts the enrichment or impoverishment of the financial balance sheet.

Organizational learning includes understanding what kind of battle is to be fought (the marketplace), the strategies to be deployed, the talent required, the skills that the talent must acquire, the level of commitment that must be fostered, and how these factors are to be orchestrated and sustained over time. This means organizational learning must take place at the executive, management, and front-line levels and must flow across functional units.

Let's look at cultural change. What happens when we ask for cultural change without learning? That is, what happens if we ask someone to do something he or she does not know how to do? We get resistance, right? Often, however, that resistance does not get expressed as a learning problem. Instead, we hear things like "bad idea," "wasn't clear," "doesn't understand how tough it is," "can't be done." We often don't know what we don't know. The root cause of most resistance is the absence of learning — learning that it needs to be done, that it can be done, and what the steps are for doing it. However, once we know it can be done (Roger Bannister runs a 4-minute mile) and know the steps — that is, learn what and how — we are in a position to acquire learning. Brain surgery is easy once you know the steps.

Management Must Lead the Learning

Market management, too, is easy once you know the steps, know its importance, and know it can be done. Without these three ingredients at executive, management, or front-line levels, the market management initiative will of course meet resistance. But if we *lead the learning* — that is, provide direction in an environment where learning is fostered — the learning will lead to cultural change. My own view is that where market management cultural change has failed, it was usually because organizational learning was conspicuously absent.

One of the primary roles of culture is to impart learning. Any attempt at cultural change, without learning, will be unsuccessful. Wal-Mart did not develop an effective discounting philosophy through serendipity. Sam Walton had a vision of being a low-cost provider, and his company planned, recruited, trained, rewarded, promoted, and terminated people according to that vision. He created a culture that *learned* at executive, management, and front-line levels how to create value through low cost and high volume.[4]

However, Wal-Mart is no more successful today than IBM, General Motors, and Sears were in their prime; they, too, were just what the marketplace wanted. As the marketplace changes and as competitors bring new alternatives, new organizational learning is needed to bring more responsive solutions. New, refined culture must now impart new, refined learning. Banks and airlines, which once had virtual monopolies, are now experiencing the same challenge. And although they have certain regulatory constraints, their biggest hurdle is *learning* how to be more market responsive. Remember George Bernard Shaw's famous quote, "Those who can, do; those who can't, teach."[5] I think we can refine it for businesses: "Those who can, do; those who can't, must learn."

In an article titled "Companies That Train Best," *Fortune* magazine describes the importance of training as a means of instituting change and organizational learning:

Concepts like empowerment, accountability, and total quality management can come off as corporate bunk if they aren't accompanied by training.[6]

Learning about the Importance of Learning

Successful companies that know the value of cultural change and organizational learning are investing in training (table 10.1). The *Fortune* article points out that every dollar Motorola spends on training delivers $30 in productivity gains within three years. Since 1987 the company has cut costs by $3.4 billion — not by the normal expedient of firing workers, but by training them to simplify processes and reduce waste. Sales per employee have doubled in the past five years, and profits have increased 47 percent.

It is ironic that when we need additional memory or a new capability for our computers, we expect to invest in software or hardware — yet when we want new functions or capabilities from our people, we are not always so clear about the relationship of investment to return. Our accounting rules don't help the cause. If we buy equipment, we amortize the depreciation over several years so that the expense "hit" to the income statement is spread out to match the expected lifetime of the benefit. In fact, with investment tax credit, it may get favorable tax treatment as well. The same money spent on training our people results in the total cost hitting the bottom line in the month of expenditure, even though the benefit will likely be spread over several years. Thus accounting and tax laws in the U.S. favor investing in things rather than people, even though the most important factors in organizational success are the skills, capabilities, and productivity of our workforce.

Pain Builds Commitment to Change

Learning is not simply giving answers; receptivity is a function of perceived relevance and need. Daryl Conner, in his book *Managing at the Speed of Change*, says that "the success of a change project depends equally on pain management and remedy selling." He states that businesses often neglect pain management.[7] We cannot

Company	Training		Comments
Number of employees worldwide	Percent of payroll spent (1992)	Avg. hours per employee per year	
Motorola 107,000	3.6%	36	The gold standard of corporate training. The company says every dollar spent on education returns $30 in productivity gains.
Target 100,000	n.a.	n.a.	Rapidly expanding retail chain has used Disney-type training to empower front-line employees & improve customer service.
Federal Express 93,000	4.5%	27	Workers take computer-based job competency tests every 6–12 months. Low scores lead to remedial action.
General Electric Aircraft Engines 33,000	n.a.	n.a.	Training budget has shrunk, but new focus on teamwork has helped the division boost productivity in a slumping industry.
Andersen Consulting 26,700	6.8%	109	Replaced 40-hour Business Practices class with interactive video, saving $4 million per year, mostly on travel & lodging.
Corning 14,000 (domestic)	3.0%	92	Ordinary employees, not professional educators, do most training. Pay of factory workers rises as they learn new skills.
Solectron 3,500	3.0%	95	Training helped this fast-growing Silicon Valley company win a Baldrige in 1991. The 1993 goal: 110 hours per worker.
Dudek Manufacturing 35	5.0%	25	Had to teach basic literacy & math before introducing quality management. Hefty investment has paid off in profits.

Table 10.1. Go to the Head of the Class

expect people to embrace the changes brought by market management if we have insulated them from the realities of the marketplace. Change and learning require energy and effort; if the status quo brings no pain, few will feel the need to change or to learn. That is why sales organizations that are focused on revenue may be blind to the increasing costs of servicing certain types of customers they have attracted. Thus they feel no imperative to change their focus.

Our challenge in market management is learning to profitably win each local market. We must analyze the specific segments and target groups that are make-or-break for us in the local trade area. We must assess our results in light of the market potential, not just based on improvement over the previous year. This requires us to develop specific approaches for providing the right sales with the right service to the right customers and prospect groups at the right cost and price. Retention, growth, attraction, and cost allocation strategies must be deployed using the corporate and local resources available. How do we learn to perform these competencies at a higher level?

TRADITIONAL APPROACHES TO MARKET MANAGEMENT

FOR MANY COMPANIES, MARKET MANAGEMENT has been neither a cultural change process nor a learning process. In fact, it has not been even a strategy, but an isolated tactic or sets of tactics without context or tie-in to a bigger picture. As one manager described it, "They asked for a plan so we gave them a plan." End of discussion. Let's look at some of the traditional tactics for change.

"Tell Them"
Many executive teams have recognized the need for a change in direction to become more responsive to unique local market needs and potential, to target certain customer groups, to reallocate costs for higher profitability. They have gathered their managers and extolled the virtues of market management, often with too few specifics on the current pain that necessitates the change.

Painting the vision is an important step; but telling someone to play center field for the Yankees is not the same as making it happen. Telling them is a little better than doing nothing — but not much. Untranslated "Executive-speak" brings little organizational change because, among other reasons, it provides almost no practical learning about market management. The branch or store manager gets little information about how, or even why, he or she needs to change tasks and routines, starting tomorrow.

"Give Them a New Title"

A second step has often been to change the store manager's title to market manager: "Because market management is so important, effective immediately your new title is market manager. We want you to go out and win your trade area. We want you to eat the competition for breakfast. You are empowered to do whatever it takes to be the provider of choice. Tier, target, segment, differenti-ate — biff, boom, bah! Any questions? Just do it!" And the managers nod approvingly and the executives checks off "market manage-ment" on their "to do" list.

By the next day, the managers have returned to their offices and to their senses. They are like the guy in the old Federal Express commercial who responds to all of his boss's demands with, "I can do that, I can do that, I can do that," then hangs up the phone and with a look of panic on his face says, "How am I going to do that?"

They try to remember what was said. "Gee, I got this new title, market manager. And let's see, was it segment, tier and then target, or was it tier, segment and then target?" They look at the stack of phone calls to return, the piles of mail, the lines of customers, the angry client waiting in the lobby, the two staff members coming down the hall with that look of urgency. And they think, "This new job sure feels like the job I had yesterday."

What's wrong with this picture? What's missing? In a word, *learning*. A change in title helps send a message as to what is expected. But as honest Abe Lincoln said, "Saying it is so doesn't make it so." If title changes did it, pro football teams would just

declare themselves Super Bowl champions at the beginning of training camp and then just wait for the big victory party in January.
Titles do not provide a new way of viewing or doing the business,
particularly when people are thrust right back into an environment
where the goals, processes, information, and rewards have not changed.

Reengineering the way we target, sell, and service customers
is not just a minor tweak. As Thomas Davenport points out in his
book *Process Innovation: Reengineering Work Through Information
Technology:*

> Process innovation can be distinguished from *process improve-
> ment*, which seeks a lower level of change. If process innovation
> means performing a work activity in a radically new way,
> process improvement involves performing the same business
> process with slightly increased efficiency or effectiveness. . . .
> Even the best American performers in terms of quality (i.e., the
> highest scores in the Baldrige award competition) improve
> reliability, cycle time, inventory turns, and so forth an average
> of only 5 percent to 12 percent; firms undertaking process
> innovation could not afford to be satisfied with these results.[8]

Where market management falls on the improvement-
innovation continuum is open to debate. Our company's experience
is that both the degree of change and the results produced indicate
that it is toward the innovation end of the scale — and the further
it moves in that direction, the more absolute is the need for new
learning. The change required is substantiative, not cosmetic. Titles
will not cause substantive change.

"Send More Reports"

A third way of instituting market management is to send more
information, on the theory that if local managers have the right data
(market research, local trade area demographics, customer profitability, target group buying motives), superior market management
will emerge. Such information is useful, but it is like sending
ammunition to soldiers who have no guns. The root cause of the
market management challenge is not a data problem. In fact, no
matter how loudly managers complain about management

information, the quality of the data available in marketing almost always exceeds the quality of the questions coming from the field.

There are always areas where better management information is needed; but the bottom line is that we are not using the information we have now. There is a small sign just outside the Holland Tunnel that connects New York City with New Jersey: "He builded better than he knew." The sign stands as a tribute to Clifford Holland, who played a key role in the excavation and construction of the tunnel, and to his ability to use and apply all the available knowledge, skills, and resources he possessed to do the best possible job. If only we could market manage "better than we know."

It has also been our company's experience that once key questions are formulated in the quest for more effective management of the local market, there is almost always a way to get an answer that can lead to better decisions. Even though the answer may be approximate, simply asking the question adds focus and insight. Peter Drucker, in an article for *The Wall Street Journal* titled "Be Data Literate — Know What to Know," asserts that every business manager must identify what questions are central to running his business and then seek out the best available form of that information:

> The data users, whether executive or professional, have to decide what information to use, what to use it for and how to use it.[9]

Local managers often have access to more information than they know how to use. The missing ingredient is the help they need in learning the right questions to ask in order to be market masters. Without that learning, they will be overwhelmed with the sheer quantity of information. They will drown in it — and yet they will be lacking the specific information they need to manage, not because it does not exist, but because without knowing the right questions they cannot sift through the heap to find the nuggets they need.

"Ask for Plans"

Finally, in an attempt to profitably win the local markets, many businesses have asked their managers to draw up local market plans. Although developing such plans is an important step in installing market management, they seldom effect cultural change. Why? If there has been no insight or innovation, then what we get, by and large, is a plan for the status quo — "Garbage in, garbage out," in computer talk. The term that comes to my mind is "pooled ignorance." Many a plan our company has seen fits that description — a proposal to keep doing the wrong stuff.

Plans developed without new business processes, tools, and skills can be awfully inconsistent. As one head of retail for a major regional bank who tried this approach lamented, "The plans I received ranged in length from 2 pages to 100 pages." Such results indicate a lack of common understanding in which time is wasted trying to figure out "what they want" rather than assessing the market. If you asked each of your managers to come up with his or her own plan for Total Quality Management without instruction on the process, practices, and philosophy of TQM, the results would only scratch the surface of the body of knowledge that has evolved over several decades. Local market management is no different.

A second fallacy is the assumption that the simple act of planning can create impetus for cultural change, organizational learning, behavior modification, new ways of thinking, new skills sets, and different results. What actually happens is that people drop what they are doing, work on the plan, get it done, hand it in — then breathe a sigh of relief and quickly resume business as usual. The plan gathers dust on a shelf because it was viewed as a unilateral, one-time event. Market plans prepared in this manner are rarely integrated into budgets, quarterly reviews, or annual goals.

The missing ingredient is learning. If merely creating plans could guarantee results, pro football teams would never practice — they would just sit in the locker room and make up game plans. But execution requires learning, spending time developing knowledge, skill, and execution.

Let's keep to the point — cultural change. If telling them, changing their titles, sending reports, and asking for plans won't bring it, what will? Learning will. Effective learning does two things: it teaches us what to do, and it provides impetus to do it.

THE PHASES OF IMPLEMENTATION

LIKE ALMOST EVERYTHING WE HAVE DISCUSSED IN THIS BOOK, the cultural change process for market management has phases. Unfortunately, these phases do not usually represent a planned approach to cultural change. Instead, executive teams take the change process as far as they can, and then — lacking the wherewithal to break into a mature, market-managed culture — get stuck.

Phase 1: "There's a Problem."
In the first phase of the cultural change, the company embraces the concept of market management. Usually this decision is based on studies that have pointed out how much profit is being made from top customers, how much is being lost off others, how different the market is from one trade area to another, and how much silent erosion is occurring. These studies may be carried out internally or externally, or they may be provided by industry groups for the entire industry. Reports, articles, books, and speakers may bring additional insights and a sense of urgency. As table 10.2 indicates, this gets us to Phase 1 — Talking. The products of this stage may be

Phase 1	Phase 2	Phase 3	Phase 4
Talk			
Study			
Change in direction			
Pronouncement of strategy			

Table 10.2. Implementation, Phase 1: Talking

Phase 1	Phase 2	Phase 3	Phase 4
Talk	Plan		
Study	Market Manager title		
Change in direction	Local market data		
Pronouncement of strategy	Market analysis & plan		

Table 10.3. Implementation, Phase 2: Planning

additional study, a change in direction by top management, and perhaps pronouncement of a market management strategy.

The key to Phase 1 is defining the problem. Once the executives start talking about the problem, there are usually two camps in the company. One group is excited about dealing with the problem: "It's about time." The second group hopes the executives "get over it" and that they are not required to do anything about it. It seems overwhelming; just thinking about it makes them tired.

Phase 2: "There's a Solution."

In Phase 2, steps are taken to translate the new direction and market management strategy into action (table 10.3). It is here that the market manager title is likely to be bestowed on area or local managers, local market data are dispensed, and local market plans are requested. These activities are carried out with insight and excitement by a few managers, but with dutiful compliance by most others. Management usually feels pretty good about what it has done at this stage. "We studied the problem and took action." They now await the good news.

Phase 1	Phase 2	Phase 3	Phase 4
Talk	Plan	Empower	
Study	Market Manager title	Natural market managers succeed	
Change in direction	Local market data	Others struggle	
Pronouncement of strategy	Market analysis & plan	Lack of trust	

Table 10.4. Implementation, Phase 3: Empowering

Phase 3: "Go for It."

In Phase 3, managers are empowered to make decisions and to take action regarding how best to meet the needs of their local markets (table 10.4). In this phase the natural market managers exceed expectations, and their results make exciting news. Others, who don't understand how to change the way they do business and who lack analysis and planning processes and the tools and skills to carry out their plans, fail. In essence, they lack a mechanism for implementation. As top management watches its managers struggle and make poor decisions, they begin to have doubts about empowerment, and in some cases, about market management. The organization perceives this doubt and loses trust in management's commitment to empowerment. The outcome is often a debate on what the problem is; some say poor strategy, others say bad implementation, incapable managers, not enough time. Paralysis can immobilize the whole company while opposing factions slug it out.

Phase 4: "Prepare for Success."

It is in Phase 4 that the organization truly gets prepared for success (table 10.5). The company invests in learning, roles are clarified, the process is defined, tools and templates are provided, and training ties it all together.

Too often, Phase 4 is implemented only after Phases 1–3 have failed, when talking, planning, and empowering have been tried with very little *enabling*. For those serious about cultural change, this sequence is wrong. Enabling is the key to facilitating learning and change. Enabling means providing processes, tools, and training to perform the new job. It should precede, or at least accompany, empowerment for two reasons. First, by failing to properly prepare for success, we may hobble our strategy, lose valuable momentum, and put the whole endeavor at risk. What went wrong may not be apparent: Was the strategy flawed? Was the implementation poor? Was it a local manager problem?

This brings us to a common dilemma that executive teams often discuss. What if some of our managers are incapable of making it as market managers? Their questions remind me of a T-shirt I once saw:

> You can't teach a pig to sing. If you try, you will become frustrated and you'll just irritate the pig.

The temptation is to let concerns about adequate talent keep the company from moving forward. To do so is a mistake. Our advice is simple. If you have someone who is failing in the job, as currently defined, take appropriate action. However, if your concern is whether all your managers can become market managers, take them through the implementation process, train them, then hold

Phase 1	Phase 2	Phase 3	Phase 4
Talk	Plan	Empower	Enable
Study	Market Manager title	Natural market managers succeed	Roles refined
Change in direction	Local market data	Others struggle	Processes/ tools/training
Pronouncement of strategy	Market analysis & plan	Lack of trust	Front-line involvement & follow-up

Table 10.5. Implementation, Phase 4: Enabling

them accountable. Some managers will raise their hands and opt out. Others will surprise you and do better than you expect. Some will do great; some will not be up to the challenge. However, to assume they cannot perform, before providing the learning and enabling, is not fair to managers and will jeopardize organizational trust.

The second reason to enable before implementing is to accelerate the payoff (fig. 10.1). Moving more quickly to the enabling step improves the success of cultural change and brings a faster (cycle time) and higher-quality payoff ("Do it right the first time").

Cultural change is our objective, and the most crucial factor in cultural change is organizational learning. This is why enabling should precede empowering. Empowerment works poorly for animals raised in captivity who are suddenly thrust into the wild.

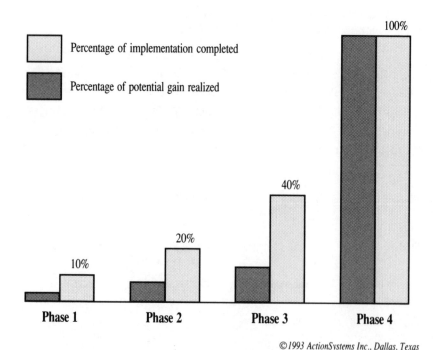

© 1993 ActionSystems Inc., Dallas, Texas

Figure 10.1. How Early Enabling Accelerates Payoff

It also has a mixed track record for managers who have operated in a regulated or near-monopolistic environment but are suddenly thrust into a highly competitive, free market. We can understand the challenges of enabling former Soviet-bloc countries to compete in the world market.

Knowing this, we must ask ourselves, What have I done as an executive or manager to manage the change? Have I articulated a strategy? Set and tracked goals? Trained? Provided a process? Developed tools? Organized teams? Have I established a game plan for managing change? In short, have I managed the learning?

What about reorganizing, changing the organizational structure? Certainly this is an important variable to consider, and it may even help — but it is not enough. Rearranging the boxes on the organizational chart is easy; changing how people think and do business is hard. It is easier to reengineer structure than process, easier to reengineer process than culture; yet structure and process work only when we reengineer or change the culture.

Regardless of our structure, old habits must be broken and significant organizational learning must take place. We are in a more competitive, market-dominated environment than ever before. To implement market management, we must enable the organization by doing three things.

One, we must sharpen our thinking and our understanding of how business must operate in this new environment. I believe market management provides this understanding. Much of this book so far has dealt with this new business theory.

Two, we must translate this thinking down, level by level, to the new business practices, tools, and skills required in a local trade area to profitably win the local market. In our experience, there are four crucial building blocks that provide the foundation for this thinking. Chapter 11 is devoted to these building blocks.

Three, we must define a process by which these building blocks — the understanding, business practices, tools, and skills — are installed into an organization. Chapter 12 will deal with this process.

11

Anchoring the Change

The Underpinnings of Market Management

66 I guess my own experience has taught me that the profound solutions to the deepest human problems must wait until we have tried the more superficial answers involving our own clever manipulations. **99** [1]

— *Keith Miller*

ONE OF THE LESSONS LEARNED IN VIETNAM was the debilitating effect of an undeclared war. A withdrawal or an attack is easier to understand and manage than a holding action. Implementing market management is a way of mobilizing for attack — a declaration of war. Like a military initiative, it implies that there will be a series of individual battles with specific strategies, troops, equipment, and tactics.

This chapter presents the four key building blocks that must be put in place once the company has decided to unleash its resources in a market-by-market assault. Our purpose here will be to identify and describe these components. Subsequent chapters will discuss the routines, practices, and processes for putting them in place.

THE CRITICAL SUCCESS FACTORS

IN IDENTIFYING THESE COMPONENTS, it is important to remember our objective. We want cultural change that enables us to profitably win local markets. The question we must ask is, "What are the critical factors which, if present, predict market management success?" These factors must aid in managing customer and market risks of retention, growth, attraction, and cost. They must embody the three principles for breakout performers: acting local, segmenting the market, and gaining breakthrough productivity. Above all, they must foster purposeful learning to support local empowerment.

It is important to note here that executive readiness must be in place prior to the four critical building blocks (a topic that will be covered in chapter 13). These four building blocks are local market absolutes, committed team, market management process and tools, and local market tactics.

BUILDING BLOCK 1: LOCAL MARKET ABSOLUTES

There are four risks in every local trade area. First, there is the risk we will not *retain* key customers; second, the risk that we will not penetrate and *grow* the right target groups; third, the risk of *attracting* the wrong prospects or no prospects; and fourth, the risk of being too *costly* in selling and servicing customers and prospects. We have discussed these risks and opportunities in the preceding chapters. They represent the absolute fundamentals of managing a local market; they are to market management what pitching, hitting, fielding, and base running are to baseball.

Retaining "Make-or-Break" Customers

Because they are so fundamental in their importance, there must always be retention strategies in place for each local trade area. That means we must have a retention strategy for each group of customers who are "make or break" for us — the ones whose loss would significantly hurt the business. We put them on our "watch list"; we monitor them as we would someone who owes us money. For each customer on the list, we should have a contact management game plan that outlines the number of on-site visits, telephone contacts, notes (birthday, anniversary as a customer, special interests), letters, and joint calls; we should have a profile system that includes background information, account history, service preferences, goals, competitive information, and our account plan. Many businesses are installing automated key-account management systems that greatly improve the quality and reduce the time for the profiling, account planning, and contact management of key customers, ensuring that more of them are proactively managed and retained. Such a system also preserves the company's memory of key customer information regardless of the turnover of people assigned to their accounts. Our company has worked with clients who were installing this software technology, and it can be a very powerful tool for managing these "make-or-break" customers.

An effective retention plan ensures that a senior staff person is assigned to manage the accounts of designated customers and to conduct periodic account reviews to keep information current. We formally assess our risk for defection or account erosion quarterly, and track fluctuations in sales, balances, and fees at specified intervals. We have learned what individual customers consider valuable and have tailored our service to those preferences. For example, if we need to provide alternatives for quick access or delivery, we may ask the customer to call on her car phone on the way to the store or branch so we can assure her of responsive assistance with no wait, or we may deliver items to the customer's office or home.

If this sounds like preferred service, it is. Several industries already have such programs in place. Airlines have frequent-flier programs for the top 1 percent; retailers designate relationship customers; banks employ private banking services. Yet in many cases, the established program does not fully respond to the unique wants and needs of local customers. For example, many high-deposit retail banking customers do not wish to be served by private banking. Some do not wish to pay the additional fees, others do not want to switch bankers, and some eschew status and image or don't want others to know of their wealth. On the other hand, some customers would be delighted to make use of these services, but no one has ever inquired or discussed the options with them. Either way, if we get it wrong, we risk losing customers.

This level of service is for a select few. In a store with 5,000 customers, personalized account management may be appropriate only for the top 1 percent (50 customers) or fewer; in others, the top 5 percent (250 customers). This decision can be aided by corporate guidelines applied locally.

Let's look at how Staples, the office supply giant, applies a segmented retention strategy. Treacy and Wiersema describe it this way:

> Staples achieves the lowest net-landed cost in the entire office stationery business, but it also has become intimate with a particular market: companies employing fewer than 50 people. To further the intimacy with that market segment, it has created a club. Customers join it at no cost and get at least a 5 percent discount on the fastest-moving items. But to get the discount, customers have to show their club card, which means Staples can track sales by customer, and that gives the company all kinds of data it can use in satisfying its market. Store managers now have incentives based on customer retention.[2]

There are many options for developing and applying retention strategies, but failure to have one should not be one of them.

Growth — Getting a Greater "Share of Wallet"

Growth, or penetration, is similar to retention. We usually target growth in customers who do some business with us, but for whom we believe there is significant potential and for whom we think cross-sell and upsell efforts have a high probability for success. As with our retention customers (most of whose business we already have), we know exactly who is on the list, why, what goals are appropriate, which person is responsible for upselling or cross-selling, which products we think will fit, what joint calling effort will be required, and what the payoff will be to the company. It is important to work with other parts of the organization for cross-sell opportunities. At American Express, for example, it would be selling financial planning and investment services to card holders; in a bank, promoting investments and trust services to affluent small-business owners.

As we set goals and track results for our salespeople, we pay close attention to their ability to convert targeted high-potential customers into high-value customers. We are pleased, of course, if they get "blue birds" elsewhere, but we track their ability to *cause* customer expansion. Are we getting additional revenue for the targeted growth accounts? We track the results as a lagging indicator, but we also track the profiling, calling activities, and sales cycles to assess, predict, and coach market penetration efforts. These are the leading indicators that forecast success or failure.

Getting the Right New Customers

Customer attraction requires the same rigor. We should have profiles of target groups we wish to bring to our business as we seek a certain market mix. We target, assign, and track prospects, and we also track conversion of prospects into customers. In many, but not all, local markets, this strategy will be less of a priority than retention and growth.

Reducing the Cost of Service Delivery to Target Groups

To free up time that we can focus on retention, growth, and attraction, we must streamline service delivery to some of our loss leaders. This, too, means we must be able to target certain groups, identify specific tactics, and in some cases develop specific lists of 10 or 20 "service hogs" who are using inordinate levels of service. In addition, we must systematically examine how we are using our time, and look for customer-driven process improvements and innovations that we can use to reengineer service delivery to make it more efficient. We must set goals, track progress, learn from our successes and failures, and reward improvement.

These four local market absolutes represent the ticket for admission to market management. In the long run, if you can't effectively manage them, you don't get to manage a market. As in the major leagues, you don't have to win every game, but eventually you must develop certain skills in pitching, hitting, defense, and base running — or the privilege gets removed. Getting the team to that level is how a manager adds value.

Any company executive should be able to walk into a branch, store, or center and within five minutes have the following information:

- Retention, growth, attraction, and cost strategies and goals
- Customers or prospects on each list
- The salesperson or account manager assigned to each high-value or high-potential customer
- Activity to date vs. the plan
- Results and trends through prior months

BUILDING BLOCK 2: THE COMMITTED TEAM

LOCAL MARKET STRATEGY ABSOLUTES TELL US *WHAT* MUST BE DONE; the committed team is *who* must do it. Throughout history, no principle of warfare has been more consistently proven: the battle is won or lost based on the commitment of its soldiers. The level of commitment required for the change to market management is certainly higher than that required for the status quo. No matter how brilliant our strategy, the results will be disappointing if we are unable to gain commitment.

Dr. Paul S. Nadler, who frequently writes for the *American Banker*, tells the story of a consultant who was working with a hotel chain on one of their most important market segments — repeat business travelers.[3] The consultant recommended an enhancement to the management information system (MIS) that would identify guests who had stayed previously at the hotel. This would allow the check-in clerk to acknowledge them and welcome them back to the hotel. The hotel chain thought the recommendation was a good one, but after much consideration, determined that the cost would be too great and nixed the idea.

About a year later, the consultant happened to be working in the same city and, as luck would have it, returned to the same hotel that he had stayed in when conducting the study for the chain. He arrived by taxi, the bellman helped him get his belongings, and he proceeded to the front desk. He gave his name to the clerk and told her that he had a reservation. She smiled and said, "Welcome back, Mr. Smith. It's good to have you with us again."

The consultant did a bit of a double take and with slight amazement inquired, "How did you know I stayed here before?"

With a twinkle in her eye, she explained. "Well, that's an interesting story. Several months ago we heard that we were going to get a new MIS system that would tell us if guests had stayed with us before so we could welcome them back. Well, I guess it cost too much or something. Anyway, we didn't get it. We were really excited about the idea, and so when it fell through, we got together and came up with our own system. You may have noticed that as you were helped by the bellman in getting your stuff out of the taxi, he asked you if you had stayed with us before."

The consultant nodded as he recalled the bellman's first question after his initial greeting. The clerk continued, "Well, when you stepped up to the counter, he set down your bags, stepped behind you, and tugged on his ear. And I said, 'Welcome back.'"

Nadler's story provides a wonderful example of a committed team in a market-management culture.

Your Sustainable Competitive Advantage

In fact, when we think of change initiatives that will make us more market driven, we can think in terms of two axes (fig. 11.1). On the vertical axis are the corporate programmatic initiatives, usually managed centrally, that provide the information, tools, and infrastructure for supporting local market management. On the horizontal axis are the cultural initiatives applied locally by focused, committed, skilled workers who truly "get it." When we build a local team to profitably win a local market, it becomes a sustainable competitive advantage. Competitors can buy profitability systems, customer information systems, and market research, and no matter how good ours is, they can always match us in three to six months. But a market management culture, one that learns to use a "tug on

Central Programmatic Initiatives

- Customer profitability model
- Customer information system
- Micro-segment research

- Market-focused vision
- Committed team
- Differentiated service for local target groups

Local Cultural Initiatives

©1993 ActionSystems Inc., Dallas, Texas

Figure 11.1. Change Initiatives

the ear," is more difficult to come by. A local market team that knows its target markets, that is constantly improving and innovating to be the provider of choice for those markets, is the most powerful weapon available. We have been surprised again and again at how resourceful local market teams can be in coming up with tug-on-the-ear solutions to make up for a lack of programmatic answers.

Building a Committed Team

As managers, our job is to create the premier market-driven culture in the local trade area. How do we create this committed team? Our company's experience indicates that there are three key variables that interact to make it happen. We will discuss these variables one at a time.

Defining roles and accountability up front. The first requirement is to define the roles and accountability of the local store. What does market management require in terms of local authority, decision-making, and empowerment? What are the "by Gods," the decisions that must be made centrally and that are not up for negotiation market by market? Clearly defining these issues saves managers a lot of time and aggravation. Nothing is more discouraging for a manager than to think she is empowered to make a decision, only to have the rug jerked out from under her. Things that are untouchable locally usually include company logos, product development, and shared management information systems.

Identifying the negotiables is equally crucial. These represent not only empowerment but responsibility and accountability for local managers making recommendations and decisions on key issues to win their local markets. Examples of negotiable issues might include hours, in-store promotions, staff assignments, and differentiated service options for target groups. Once these boundaries between central and local authority are clear, energy and attention can be focused on profitably winning the local market. These key accountabilities are the raw material from which retention, growth, attraction, and cost reduction are produced.

In effect, we are asking some managers to sign up for a new job — a job that to some extent has just been invented. Others we are simply asking to get better at something they are already doing. If roles, responsibilities, and accountabilities are not well defined, we can expect confusion and poor performance. However, defining roles need not be an overwhelming task. Often a day-long role clarity session with managers and executives can define and document their roles. Then we use the implementation process to install these roles, responsibilities, and accountabilities. In some companies, changes in roles and accountabilities are relatively conservative in year one, with more occurring in years two and three.

Involving and empowering managers and the front line. It's simple: market management is not something done *to* local teams, but *by* and *with* them. If we are serious about gaining their commitment, we must involve them in market analysis, planning, and implementation. Not only does involvement build commitment, it also fosters learning.

There are certainly quicker, more efficient means of preparing market plans than involving each local team member, but let's go back to the central issue: cultural change. We cannot gain their commitment, energy, intellect, and innovation if we do not involve them.

These are all wonderful reasons for involvement and empowerment, but they are not the most compelling. Why are companies such as Xerox, Motorola, Chrysler, General Electric, and AT&T eliminating layers of management, authorizing workers to make decisions, implementing local work teams? It is because, if enabled, they can often make and implement decisions more quickly, more effectively, and more efficiently. Let's look at specifics:

- Who knows the identity of the ten to twenty service hogs in a local branch/store/center?
- Who makes decisions daily about how long to spend with each customer?

- Who best knows where service delivery is not working?
- Who sees the expression on a customer's face during a service "moment of truth"?
- Who has friends and family relationships within the local customer base?
- Who is most likely to live in the local trade area?
- Who has friends that work for the competition?
- Who best understands the needs and wants of our target groups?

Our front-line managers and staff are not perfect, but they are our richest resource — a virtual gold mine of market data. We must mine this gold. Use it or lose it!

Providing skill development and learning. Without skill development and learning, empowerment and accountability are a cruel joke. We've talked a lot about learning, but let's look at it in relationship to commitment. If we are not continually demonstrating our commitment by developing our people, their learning and skills will become obsolete. This leads us ultimately to one of two choices: either we figure out that they lack the skills for success and therefore withhold empowerment, or we empower them anyway but they fail because of their skill deficiencies. In either case, we create an environment of failure and blame.

The single greatest reason for failure in implementing market management is the absence of a learning mechanism for front-line managers and staff. Millions of dollars are invested in market data, profit models, customer information systems, customer service surveys, and strategic studies to analyze the problem. Nothing is spent to teach people the mindset, knowledge, and skills to operate in the new environment. In military terms, it would be like transitioning from hand-to-hand combat to tank warfare, buying tanks and tank artillery but not training the troops in tank operations, field tactics, maintenance or repair. Either market management is genetic or it must be learned. It is not genetic — and the results in many companies say it has not been learned.

Obviously roles and accountabilities, involvement and empowerment, and skill development are related, and obviously there are other factors that impact commitment; the ones discussed are those my colleagues and I have found most relevant.

One final point on empowerment. Some are skeptical about local market empowerment. In our consulting experience, much of the skepticism is warranted, because many executives know deep down that their business has thrived in an environment of following orders. They also know that theirs is not a learning organization, and because they have not prepared people to win their local markets, they are not optimistic about success through empowerment. As we look across a broad range of industries, it seems more and more clear that the old command-and-control structure is too slow, too expensive, and too unresponsive to win in today's environment and will eventually go the way of the dinosaur. David Nadler, president of Delta Consulting Group, describes this as the first stage of decomposition of the corporation.[4]

Quick, responsive, productive local market teams are at the core of local market effectiveness. Building commitment through accountability, empowerment, and development is a critical part of the foundation for building effective market management teams.

BUILDING BLOCK 3: PROCESSES AND TOOLS

A COMMITTED TEAM NEEDS TOOLS. The more significant the change, the more crucial the need. Tools provide leverage for an intended outcome. Given time, committed teams will develop tools on their own. However, there are risks with leaving teams to their own devices.

Many of our front-line managers and staff are not capable of inventing the tools needed to implement market management. That is not what they are good at. Most are implementers, not inventors. They have good ideas and valued insight, but their roles, time requirements, and skills preclude their developing a set of world-class tools. If our best performance is a function of the tools they can develop, we unnecessarily limit our potential.

In many cases the tools developed are crude and inadequate for the task. After much effort, the team gives up. They needed a shovel; they got a spoon. Inadequate or defective tools may be worse than nothing. If the effort of analyzing the market, developing a plan, tiering accounts, and managing key accounts is too great, people will eventually give up and revert to old practices. Committed troops without weapons, supplies, or ammunition can take us only so far. It is very inefficient to stop in the midst of "war" to create tools, and redundant to have each unit reinvent the wheel.

What we need are the best tools available, tools that reflect state-of-the-art, breakthrough approaches that can be tailored to fit the company's structure, strategy, systems, and skills. Three types of tools are needed to support a committed team in installing market management: processes, templates, and skills.

A Step-by-Step Process

The local unit needs a road map showing how to analyze its market effectively and efficiently, develop a plan, and implement retention, growth, attraction, and cost management strategies to profitably win its local market. The process must promote understanding, learning, and action in a way that removes obstacles to cultural change. Executives need a process to prepare the company for the change. Staff roles such as marketing, finance, systems, and human resources need a process to help them create the data, marketing, and people solutions to support change in general and local market plans in particular.

The acid test for the process is that it must accomplish all these things elegantly. Complexity invites inaction. The process must do complex things in a simple way, without collapsing under its own weight.

Templates

Process outlines the steps for moving to market management; templates make the steps easy, quick, and consistent. Templates are tools in their purest form. They provide "fill-in-the-blank" mechanisms — a common set of questions — for assessing the trade area, identifying target markets, creating a segment-specific tactical plan. "Snap-on" templates measure and track results.

Effective templates help franchise the business; everyone operates from the right questions, and over time they become institutionalized. Market to market, the questions are the same — but the answers are different.

Effective templates are a key weapon in the battle for speed to market. They can double or triple the quality and speed of a committed team in applying market management. If cycle time matters, templates are crucial.

The Right Skill Set

For effective use of processes and tools, it is important to determine what skills are needed to do the job. These skills can be separated into two broad types: one, the skills required for conducting market analysis and planning — sizing the market, tiering customers, assessing the competition, and so forth; two, the day-to-day delivery skills of providing differentiated service to target customers, streamlining service delivery, and upselling targeted high potentials, to name a few.

Many skill needs can be supported with low-cost templates and tools — but some require training to ensure that skill deficiencies do not impair our ability to implement market management. Much of the traditional sales-and-service training has failed to deal with the segmentation and focusing of these skills to target groups.

Process, templates, and skills ensure that committed teams can perform as intended. Even companies with strong visions and committed teams sometimes fail because they neglect this job of equipping the troops.

BUILDING BLOCK 4: LOCAL MARKET TACTICS

LOCAL MARKET STRATEGY ABSOLUTES, committed team, processes, and tools — what could be missing? What is missing are some tried-and-true tactics that can be deployed once we know our objectives for target markets. For example, retention strategies may require assigning senior people to high-value customers or changing the service promise for their in-store service needs.

The 5 P's

There is a menu of known solutions that can be combined with created solutions to optimize retention, growth, attraction, and cost management in a local target market. These tactics can be organized into five categories — the 5 P's of marketing: people, premises, promotions, (service) promise, and products/pricing. Marketing departments typically use these categories (or similar ones) to define marketing.

Local market management is designed to execute these P's in the local trade area. There is an interesting corollary in the world of systems. Twenty years ago, virtually all organizational data resided on a mainframe computer at headquarters. Field offices had very little data other than what was given to them in reports. The concept of distributed processing began to encourage organizations to provide local PCs that could access needed information off the mainframe. The information was shifted to the user in the field to enhance and support local decisions.

Marketing is no different. Local market management could be called distributed marketing — that is, moving the marketing information closer to the user so that it has more value for the company and especially the customer. Distributed marketing increases the importance and value of the marketing function and makes it more consultative. Let's look at each of the 5 P's.

People. The reallocation of people to target markets is one of the cornerstones of local market management. Specific "people tactics" are needed to profitably win target markets. A menu of possibilities helps ensure that the tactics used fit the market and optimize resources. Too often, time and skill assignments are based on demand rather than profit contribution or potential.

Premises. Premise or place tactics involve hours, traffic flow, layout, customer waiting areas, and customer servicing areas. Once we stake out target markets and our specific retention, growth, attraction, and cost reduction strategies, we must ask the question, "How well does our facility support the strategy?" Although major renovations or expansions are sometimes warranted, usually we make do with what we have. So how do we optimize based on our physical constraints? We design premise tactics that help us become the store of choice for our target markets.

Promotions. Head-office campaigns, contests, and promotions to push certain central initiatives, while necessary, are frequently not well suited to all local markets. What we need is local promotions that are coordinated with head-office campaigns. For instance, local high-value customer appreciation, community events, in-branch employee contests, direct mail, and other kinds of promotions can fill the gaps not addressed by head-office campaigns. The trend is toward central campaigns offered as a menu, with each local unit selecting those items that best fit their market.

Service promise. As we identify target markets, we must define the service promise that will deliver the desired results. Some preferred-client promotions have implied special service that was not delivered. What could be worse for business than raising customers' expectations but doing nothing to meet those expectations?

We must systematically define our service promise for each target group — that is, understand what customers expect from us — and then reengineer the processes that don't conform to the promise. If we promise to assign someone who understands the customer's unique situation and needs, we must do it! At the crux of these service promise tactics are the issues around differentiated service: transaction, multiproduct, or account management.

Products/pricing. We are not typically going to develop products locally, nor will we set pricing policy for the company. However, based on our target markets, we must know certain products better than others; we may have to tailor, bundle or unbundle to gain an edge; we may need to use certain relationship pricing tactics that are available to us within the pricing strategy. Often we are competing against local independent businesses, and we must make informed decisions regarding tailoring and flexing to compete.

These tactics take us to the nuts and bolts of winning a local market. Based on a review of hundreds of local market analyses and plans, our firm has developed a master list of 70 local market tactics. This master list provides a universe of possible tactics to consider, but there are usually two to four that are priority in any given local market.

To win the local market, we must commit to all four of these building blocks: local market absolutes, committed team, market management process and tools, and local market tactics; anything less defeats our purpose. However, once we commit to them, we must address how we get the building blocks in place. The first step is to identify the crucial practices that must become a way of doing business in a market-managed environment. That is the topic of the next chapter.

12

Putting It All Together

The Practices of a Market Manager

66 What makes a man a good athlete?
Practice. What makes a man a good
artist, a good sculptor, a good musician?
Practice. What makes a man a good
linguist, a good stenographer? Practice.
What makes a man a good man?
Practice. Nothing else. 99 [1]

— *Henry Drummond*

WHAT DO MARKET MANAGERS DO that is different from what traditional branch, store, or center managers do? They manage sales, service, budgets, people and so forth — but that is not what is different. As Peter Senge would ask, what have they *learned* that others haven't?

Treacy and Wiersema, in the *Harvard Business Review*, describe some of Kraft USA's local market practices in individual supermarket chain stores:

> Kraft decentralized its marketing operation in order to empower the people actually dealing with the customer . . . tailored its advertising, merchandising and operations in a single store or in several stores within a supermarket chain to the needs of those stores' particular customers . . . [and] educated its sales force to allow it to develop as many different so-called micromerchandising programs for a chain that carries its products as the chain has stores. . . . Instead of pushing one-size-fits-all sales promotion programs, Kraft salespeople worked with individual store managers and regional managers to create customized promotional programs . . . [and Kraft] provided profiles of customers who have bought particular products.[2]

Our consulting firm has spent the last five years researching this question. We have studied several industries and worked with a variety of companies in defining and installing a market management process. Again and again we have seen a set of practices that market managers have learned that differentiate them from others.

In the mid-1980s we consulted with many businesses to identify the most successful sales-and-service management practices of first-line store managers and their bosses — usually regional or area managers. In each case we asked the company to give us two to three days with five to eight of their best performers, and conducted a "success analysis" to identify what top performers do that mediocre and poor performers don't. We then developed processes, templates, and training to incorporate these best practices into the company's skill set and culture. Although our primary mission was sales-and-service management, we noticed that top performers described a set of practices that preceded sales-and-service management, that provided the foundation on which it was based. In fact, many of the traditional challenges of sales-and-service management (Why don't they coach? Why aren't they holding sales meetings? Why aren't they tracking?) seemed to stem from the absence of these foundation market management practices. If we do not have clarity on the target groups we seek, the relative emphasis on retention, growth, attraction, and cost, on the tactics that support target group strategies, we can be assured that sales-and-service management will lack specificity and probably sustainable commitment.

CONFLICTING MESSAGES ABOUT MARKET MANAGEMENT

A RECENT SURVEY BY OUR COMPANY of 35 banks with over $1 billion in assets found that 88 percent of respondents considered market management a critical strategy. But few translated this belief into coherent practices. These are some of the specifics we found:

- Only 15 percent tier their customers by relationship profitability.
- Only 5 percent set growth goals by market segment, identified and managed at the local level.
- Only 35 percent provide any market segmentation training as part of their sales-and-service strategy.
- Only 17 percent provide their managers with training to analyze market data and develop a market plan.
- Only 18 percent augment their competitive profiles with locally gathered market data.
- Only 29 percent have a strategy to differentiate service by enhancing service quality for their best customers and lowering cost of service to their least profitable customers.

To understand this current reality, we asked executives and managers about the importance and use of these practices. Some knew that their front-line managers and staff were not deploying the practices of market management. Others weren't sure, and yet others believed they were making progress.

What we were able to conclude is that —

- If you think you are not doing it, be assured you are not.
- If you are not quite sure, be assured you are not.
- If you think you are, you probably are not.
- If you know you are, you are probably making progress but have a way to go.

In spite of good intentions and, in some cases, serious progress, there are many conflicting messages that reflect the gap in implementation of market management:

- Talking about the importance of customers, but tracking only products.
- Initiating service enhancement to A customers, but doing nothing to streamline service delivery to C's.
- Cutting cost but not changing the way business is done.
- Studying segmentation, target markets, and customer profitability while goals, budgets, and annual plans of local managers ignore them all.

THE MIND SET OF A MARKET MANAGER

AS OUR COMPANY BEGAN TO PUT THE PIECES TOGETHER, we identified a series of practices that define market management. This chapter outlines those practices. First, however, it is important to understand the four critical questions that must be a part of the manager's mind set for the practices to be relevant. In essence, the practices are designed to provide answers to these four questions.

Critical Question 1: What Is Your Market Potential?

Your job as a market manager is to wring out the profit potential that is available in your local market. This job description is different from the traditional "Increase revenue by 10 percent over last year," to use one example. The difference between being driven by the potential in a market and being driven by the history of sales growth is subtle but profound. In a growing market, 10 percent over last year might be pathetic; in a shrinking market, maintaining the same performance as last year may be monumental. Not everyone has a market where 10 or 15 percent growth is realistic; the beauty of market management is that everyone has the opportunity to optimize local market potential.

"Sizing the market" means defining how big is "big" — or how small is "small." Should you expand? Should you shrink? Should you be here at all? Certain head office directives regarding corporation-wide targeted segments or profit targets may mean that you have no business being in a given local market because it does not fit the strategy. However, if the market fits the strategy, you can view your job as realizing the local market potential. This increases accountability, because it is based on local realities of customers, prospects, and competitors, not just a corporate reality of, say, average growth needed across all markets. It is important to recognize that in a number of cases this makes the goals more rigorous because the potential warrants it.

Critical Question 2: Who Are Your Priority Target Groups?

When you size any local market, it becomes apparent that there are two or three predominant target groups whose business is essential to you. These groups are so important that, no matter how well you do elsewhere, you cannot profitably win your local market without them.

A market manager, regardless of revenue or profits to date, knows there must be committed, focused attention on these target groups if the local franchise is to grow and succeed. This does not mean ignoring other customer groups — it means applying incremental resources to these target groups. Nor does it mean that product volume or overall profits become less important, but that your focus should be on these target groups as a priority for meeting volume and profit goals.

Critical Question 3: How Do You Profitably Retain and Grow Existing Relationships, Attract New Target Group Customers, and Manage Costs?

The third question begins with "How?" Once you know *who* your target markets are, *how* will you become the provider of choice for them? Here is where you apply the four strategies (retention, growth, attraction, cost reduction) and the five tactics (five P's) to make it happen. The quintessential market manager moves beyond macrogoals of revenue growth and profits; she targets where these will come from, and how. And she is particularly interested in the leading indicators that predict success — the essential skills and activities that will eventually *cause* sales and service to profitably win the local market.

Critical Question 4: How Do You Build and Execute an Integrated Market Plan to Quantify and Achieve the Desired Financial Outcomes?

What is your mechanism for managing your local market intentions? You need a plan that documents your market goals, the financial impact of meeting those goals, how you expect to get it done, and what you will "inspect" or pay attention to along the way.

The plan and the tracking will be necessary to keep you on course during "distraction attacks." All the good ideas and energy must be organized and harnessed. You must tap creativity and empowerment, *and* you must not be done in by chaos and inconsistency.

These four questions must precede the practices, or else you have answers (practices) for which there are no questions or context. The move to market management is not born of compliance; it is born of insight, energy, learning, empowerment, and accountability.

CRITICAL PRACTICES OF A MARKET MANAGER

ONCE THESE FOUR QUESTIONS HAVE BEEN ANSWERED, market management practices become essential enablers for quickly and effectively transforming the organization. We will talk about three key steps in this transformation, and we will discuss some of the subcomponents of each. These practices, and the tools and training that support them, will vary across industries and in fact must be customized for each company. Our discussion will provide more detail than some of you want, while others will want more explanation than we give here. Our objective is to provide an overview without getting into the details that differ among companies and industries.

Step One: Market Analysis

Becoming a student of your market. Once war has been declared and the troops have either volunteered or been drafted, there is an important orientation phase to help people understand the concepts and principles of market management. With that step out of the way, you are now ready to focus on market analysis.

Market analysis is designed to answer that first question: "What is my market potential?" It requires you to look *outside* your unit at the total potential of your trade area, and it requires you to look *inside* at the potential within your existing customer base.

Looking outside: What do the numbers tell you? As you look outside, you must first define your trade area, then identify the available quantitative data sources that will tell you about the prospective customer base. The objective is to size the market so you will know *what* the potential is, and with *whom*. For a seller of office products, you might need information on the number of businesses in your trade area. You might also want to know the number of corporate or regional offices there, because that may be where buying decisions are made. For a clothing store that specializes in children's wear, the number of households with children (preferably by age categories) would be important.

The details of how local market data and competitive information are collected and analyzed vary across industries and companies according to the quality and quantity of available data. However, market managers are often frustrated by the lack of support from their company. We can aid them greatly by providing templates and a consistent way of handling the information to enhance the speed, use, and quality of the market analysis.

Many companies have gathered potentially valuable information but, because of its sheer volume or the fact that most of their managers are unaware of it, are unable to analyze or use it. More importantly, if they have not made the mindshift to market management, they probably lack the right set of questions for which the data provide answers, as well as a process that gains the input and involvement of the entire local team. One market manager our consultants worked with had estimated that there were 75 small businesses in his trade area, but when he analyzed his data he found there were more than 2,000. His approach to the market had grossly undermanaged the potential. Herbert Stein is right! It ain't what people don't know that hurts, it's the things they know that ain't so.[3]

Looking inside. Analyzing the market data, analyzing the trade area, and profiling the competition all involve looking outside. As you turn your attention inside the store, you must first look at the composition of your customer base.

Tiering your customers. Your goal is to categorize or tier your customers locally in order to understand your present customer mix, its needs and its potential. In essence, you ask, "Who have we attracted?" One of the important issues at this stage is to establish the criteria for tiering, because they will greatly influence the outcome. Some businesses tier according to profit, revenue, geography, potential, demographics/psychographics, income, industry, and many other factors. In a local grocery store we get different tierings, depending on which of several factors we are concerned with: volume of purchases, highly loyal customers, customers with large households, most profitable customers, frequent shoppers, or affluent shoppers. The crucial question is, Which tiering criterion or criteria would be most useful to the store manager in profitably winning the local market? These criteria obviously should fit the company's overall strategy.

All stores or branches have informal means of tiering their customers. Too often, though, the tiering is de facto, with individual employees delivering service to whoever comes in most often, customers they like (or poor service to customers they dislike), those easiest to serve, or the most prominent, regardless of actual or potential profit contribution. By establishing a formal set of criteria and a process, however, you can make intentional and purposeful decisions on customer priorities and service delivery.

What do customers have to say about you? As your understanding of the trade area and especially the existing customer base grows, it becomes more important to understand how customers perceive the current level of service. Most businesses already assess customer feedback; your first step should be to review this existing information. However, there are two limitations that dilute its usefulness. Sometimes the information is broken down only to the regional level, making it difficult or impossible to evaluate the local branch or store.

An even larger concern is that most surveys do not show how you are doing by particular segments or target groups. In a retail bank branch where high-deposit seniors and dual-income professionals are the two most important target groups, combining their survey responses into one "average" service rating might hide the fact that seniors want you to provide a comfortable place to sit, while professionals need longer hours or Saturday banking. These responses would, in effect, cancel each other out so that neither service issue would appear to rate very high.

If you are serious about winning target groups, you must understand their unique service needs and how well you are meeting those needs. Remember that target groups are homogeneous subcategories of segments that have similar buying motives and tend to value the same things. You need quick, simple, low-cost ways of getting segmented feedback from local target groups.

What can your employees tell you? If you are interested in enhancing service to these target customers, there is another group that you must understand and appreciate — your internal customers, the people who work in the local store. Simply assessing what they like about their jobs, what they don't like, what their goals are, and what motivates them is invaluable in preparing a market plan. It can be very energizing and rewarding for both manager and staff, and it brings you back to the central point: "It's cultural change, stupid." Providing the appropriate processes, templates, and tools takes little time and generates high value. It lets you build a "market plan" for your internal customers.

Self-inspection: Taking a close look inside. When you analyze the needs of external and internal customers, you should examine local store processes. Not only do you need to eliminate problems and reengineer service to respond to the needs of key target groups, you should do the same for internal staff. Asking the staff how the process can be improved is a good way to generate customer-focused innovation and improve the staff's commitment to market-driven change.

Looking both inside and outside enables you to accomplish the key goal of market analysis: identifying and describing the target groups — both external and internal — that will be paramount to profitably winning your local markets. These groups truly serve as the bull's eye for your retention, growth, attraction, and cost management strategies and the associated tactics that will be developed as part of your market plan.

When we think of market analysis, we often focus on quantitative analysis. It's true that this is valuable — but you must keep your eye on the goal: cultural change. You cannot get change by simply telling people it is important; you must create insight as to what is possible. Most people think they are giving their best now; until they achieve this insight, their desire and ability to change will be minimal.

Effective market analysis gets the whole team thinking in terms of what is possible, envisioning potential. What if we gain another 5 percent market share in our most profitable target group? Seeing this as possible builds energy and commitment and generates ideas and plans for getting there. The team discards the old reality and picks up a new, updated reality.

It is this kind of insight that enables local teams to commit to "stretch" goals. Yet many attempt to install these goals with no process for gaining insight. The result is often passive resistance to change — and this can be deadly.

A lot of what people "know" about their local market "ain't so," and these preconceptions limit their ability to take on new challenges and to see new possibilities. That is why providing a process that helps the team embrace what is possible in the local market is the most important outcome of the local market analysis — even more important than the quantitative "right" answer. There are faster ways to get the right answer but there is not, in our experience, a quicker way to get the right behavior.

Step Two: Market Planning

Creating the road map for winning your local market. Once your analysis is complete, you need a detailed game plan for profitably winning your local market — a road map to guide weekly, monthly, and quarterly local sales-and-service routines. Too often, plans are created merely to comply with regional or corporate requests. Much of this effort is wasted motion. A plan must be a mechanism for managing weekly behavior, activities, and results. If it fails to do that, it misses the point — cultural change.

Furthermore, most plans are based on a premise of meeting revenue or profit goals. The plan should accomplish these goals; but that is not enough. You need a plan for how to dominate a market, based on market potential, and a structure for the weekly activities that will move you in small but certain steps toward attracting, retaining, and growing your targets, and ultimately dominating your market.

What are your market goals? Effective market managers establish deadlines for reaching market goals. They use their market potential analysis to chart where they are now; then they stake out where they need to be 12 months from now. This way, they manage their unit to a customer mix goal based on market potential, competition, and comparative strengths of the local staff and facilities.

The whos and hows of the plan. The rest of the plan deals with attaining the market goals. Once the market manager has specified the mix of A's, B's, and C's and which groups will be targeted within each segment, he must address *how* he will obtain this mix to win and profit in the local market. The market analysis provides the data on which to base your strategies and tactics.

The plan is built around the four local market strategy absolutes, which we call the RGAC strategies:

- Retention of key customers
- Growth of existing relationships
- Attraction of targeted prospects
- Cost reduction or reassignment of service delivery

For each strategy there are five categories of possible tactics. Most managers and staff who engage in the process do not have a mental checklist of all possible tactics, nor are they always skilled at translating the market analysis data into well-thought-out conclusions. Our experience indicates that, at this stage in the market management process, structured learning is helpful. We have formulated a series of conclusion support tools and a "decision tree" of questions that directs the manager to a specific set of tactics that fit his unique market needs.

We have also found that providing a master list of proven tactics stimulates new ideas and helps fill in the gaps for managers who may know some but not all of the possibilities. For example, customer retention tactics used by such companies as L.L. Bean have proven effective in salvaging up to 75 percent of customers who have already decided to leave. Some of the tactics persuade defectors to return; others anticipate and prevent defections. Still, some tactics must be invented for unique local requirements because the master list cannot cover every eventuality.

What's it worth? Building a business case. For each key strategy, you must specify quantitative goals: What might an improvement in the retention or growth of a target market be worth? In our earliest consulting work, we omitted this vital step. People tended to say, "Of course I can win the local market, but I need resources. We need to add people, we need more equipment, we'll expand hours, and we'll build a new wing." However, once we started requiring accountability for payback and premium on investment, the story changed dramatically. These days people often look for ways to further reduce cost and increase value, and frequently recommend halting planned expenditures and using budgets differently or not at all.

Some participants in the market management process will lament recent expenditures. In one of our recent sessions, a manager complained:

> We spent $500,000 to upgrade our store. I thought we needed it, our facilities people thought we needed it, and the general manager thought we needed it — so we did it. Three weeks into this market analysis process, I knew we had made a mistake. That very large investment created very little value for our best customers. In fact, if I am really honest, we did it for us, not for our customers. If I had spent a third of that money on more proactive, personalized consultation and service to our A customers, I would have been miles ahead.

Yes, there are times when you need to invest, but effective market analysis lets you examine the potential, calibrate the risk, and design the solution for the target market.

A final reason for the business case is to help ensure executive constancy for the cause of market management. A word to managers who need more executive support: Executives understand the benefits of empowerment, local market focus, process innovation, segmentation, and a gaggle of other terms that represent their "second language." But the mother tongue of executives who sit in the hot seat and face off directly or indirectly with shareholders and board members is *profit* and *shareholder value*. If you wish to do business in the homeland, you must speak the native tongue ("Profit" spoken here!). Define your intentions and plans in terms of bottom-line results.

We are typically seeing market plans that target approximately 10 percent profit improvement in Year 1. Yet our clients have documented numerous cases in which profits actually improved by 20, 30, or even 40 percent after local teams got truly focused and implemented local market management.

Step Three: Marching Orders for the Local Market

The Summary Market Plan. The final step begins with consolidating all these plans and tactics into a brief summary: target markets, RGAC strategies, key tactics, and profit improvement, all on a single page. As one of our clients said, "If you can't net it down to one page, you are not finished."

This Summary Market Plan describes succinctly how to profitably win the local market. It specifies the local changes that front-line managers and staff must make. It quantifies what it will be worth to the business in bottom-line results. It reflects market analysis and planning practices that lead to management by fact, sound conclusions, and strong beliefs. It assumes that these practices will be applied again and again to refine and update the plan.

If you have done it right, your analysis and planning process will promote cultural change. The new way of thinking will have already led to changes and implementation of some ideas, and to the third set of practices — the execution of the plan.

As managers and their teams create local market plans, they begin to think of themselves as stewards of their franchise, responsible for retaining and growing an income stream from targeted and prospective customers by giving them the value they want and are willing to pay for. RGAC strategies and tactics have become a common vocabulary, and each person has assumed a specific role for making it happen.

How do daily and weekly routines change? Local teams set and operate off customer and market goals. They reallocate sales-and-service efforts based on RGAC plans. "A" customers are profiled. Weekly targets are set for proactive, targeted calls. Joint calls, coaching, and reinforcement are all focused on accomplishing customer and market plans.

Market management is not a talking game, although talk is required. Nor is it an analysis game, although analysis plays an important role. Market management is an *implementation* game — and A-level implementation of a B strategy is better than B implementation of an A strategy.

The bullet question for each executive team is, "What have we done to implement and install market management as a means for changing the way we do business?" Our firm is often amazed at how a company will spend hundreds of thousands of dollars, sometime millions, to collect and analyze data, and virtually nothing to apply and implement it locally. It is as though McDonald's spent millions on research to identify customer preferences, but nothing to teach local managers and front-line people the processes, menus, and cooking skills to fulfill those preferences. With all the money being spent on strategic studies, new technology (voice response units, automation, customer profitability systems), market research, and demographic data, too little is invested in applying the know-how in the local market — that is, processes, templates, tools, practices, training, tracking, follow-up, and refresher training. If you wish to bring quality and speed to implementation, then you have to plan for and execute cultural change and learning. A market management system implemented by trial and error, invented from scratch in each local market, will be a waste time, cost, and opportunity.

We have identified the critical practices that will make market management a way of doing business. Unfortunately, there is no "market management practices pill," so we must design a process for implementing and installing the change. Most companies underestimate the challenge.

TEN COMMANDMENTS

FOR THE COMPANY SERIOUS ABOUT MARKET MANAGEMENT, there are ten commandments that summarize everything we have talked about thus far — that are, we believe, necessary for success:

Commandment 1: Implement a cultural change process, led by executive management, that promotes team building and commitment by local staff to local market plans.

Commandment 2: Provide a systematic process that sizes the local market potential and tiers existing customers into segments and target groups.

Commandment 3: Provide instruction and focus on the strategies of retention, growth, attraction, and cost management (RGAC).

Commandment 4: Teach the principles of acting local, segmenting the market, and obtaining breakthrough productivity through reallocation of resources.

Commandment 5: Create urgency for change by facilitating new insights for the local market team.

Commandment 6: Identify and apply marketing tactics of people, promotions, premises, service promise, and products/pricing to RGAC strategies in local target markets.

Commandment 7: Provide tools and templates that simplify the process and ensure a quick, consistent means for completing and implementing market plans.

Commandment 8: Incorporate executive, peer, and consultant feedback in market analysis conclusions and market plans.

Commandment 9: Implement the process vertically (one region, district or area at a time) to create alignment from executive strategy to front-line tactics/skills within 90–120 days.

Commandment 10: Set and track RGAC goals for target groups in each local trade area, created and committed to by local staff, based on studied local market plans.

13

Overcoming the Obstacles

Removing Barriers to Success

66 It is always true that the most important part of any achievement is the part that no one sees. 99 [1]

— *William Barclay*

WE KNOW THE PROBLEM; we understand the concept and the principles and the practices. Where do we start? Stephen Covey, in *The Seven Habits of Highly Successful People,* says that when we are addressing cultural change, approximately 30 percent of our efforts should go to promoting the targeted change and 70 percent should be directed at removing the obstacles.[2] I believe he is right. The road to change is best described by the obstacles we must overcome. If we can invest in truly understanding the obstacles, we can design and direct our efforts to remove or overcome as many of them as possible. Many desirable organizational initiatives bite the dust because too little attention is paid to the obstacles.

Starting with the obstacles means being committed to looking in the mirror. As a famous opossum named Pogo once said, "We have met the enemy, and he is us."[3] Regardless of whether we are executives, managers, or front-line staff, we must deal with our own preconceived notions, habits, and reluctance. If we are not willing to change the game and operate at a higher level, then the whole topic of market management is academic.

There are two kinds of obstacles that are difficult to overcome: failure — and success. Failure with previous organizational initiatives is particularly troublesome; when we try something that doesn't work — something that looked great going in — we lose energy for and confidence in the next new idea. Perhaps there is no greater obstacle to change than the fact that doing something new and different takes energy, a commodity in short supply in companies that have been through a lot of change. Energy is often low after mergers, consolidation, downsizing, restructuring, or reorganization; it is not replenished when the change is perceived as overly painful or unsuccessful. As one manager recently asked in a market analysis and planning session, "If we are doing so good, how come it feels so bad?" Even when we win, it doesn't always feel like it.

Success can also be a major stumbling block, because it doesn't create urgency for change. It challenges us in two ways. First, success is a lagging indicator; the success we experience today was probably caused by things we did six to eighteen months ago. Second, we often draw wrong conclusions about what causes success (and failure).

So as we approach the next level in our climb to market management, we should systematically assess the obstacles. If we are prepared, removing obstacles can give us great impetus toward success.

In this chapter we identify the most common, but not all, of the obstacles to breakthrough market management. Although they overlap, we have organized them into two categories: executive, for those the executive team must overcome; and management, for those to be surmounted by managers.

OBSTACLES FOR EXECUTIVES

AS WE EXAMINE THE OBSTACLES FOR EXECUTIVES, the first three deal with getting started. These obstacles cost us precious cycle time in a war where absence of speed kills.

Obstacle One: "We're Already Doing It! (I Think. Aren't We?)"

In our initial consultations, we often hear executives say that they think their stores, branches, or centers are already practicing market management. To some extent, they are correct. But are they doing it well enough to win — and keep winning? A retail executive for one of the top five U.S. banks recently explained it this way:

> We have been talking about managing local markets around here for two or three years. But until we actually put in a process, tools and skills, we had only scraped the surface. Now, we have really begun to walk the walk.

The incongruity between what enlightened management would like to do and what is actually happening day in and day out in local stores stems from the fact that most businesses do not have a working model for competing at the local level.

A few exceptional managers, maybe 5 to 10 percent, are pretty good at market management and can get better. But for the majority — unless you have installed a process for market analysis, planning and implementation with specific practices for retention, growth, attraction, and cost management targeted against specific target groups; unless you have dramatically reallocated time, staff, and other resources branch by branch or store by store based on local market potential; unless you have provided a learning system that enables the local franchise manager and her staff to become market masters — our experience would say that you have not institution-alized market management. And denying this reality only obstructs progress toward a solution. If you wait long enough, you will see a clear vision of market management — from your competitors.

Obstacle Two: "We'll Do It When Things Settle Down."

This statement acknowledges a very real problem. With too many unrelated initiatives coming at them, front-line people may be over-whelmed by the changes needed for market management — and underwhelmed with the executive team's ability to make them understandable, relevant, and strategically meaningful.

What is often much less clear is that market management is an outstanding mechanism to break the cycle, to regain control of the business. The reason that things are so unsettled is that, without market management, you are at the mercy of all of those sales, service, cost, and market initiatives coming at you randomly. Since none of them single-handedly addresses the whole problem, you can always assume that there will soon be another initiative to address the parts of the problem that were neglected. It's easy to get stuck in a self-perpetuating cycle; as in the oft-faxed cartoon, "The flogging will continue until morale improves."

Changing the game may be the only way to settle things down. You need a mechanism that helps you gain control and focus in a very dynamic marketplace with emerging, ever-changing com-petitors and market needs.

Obstacle Three: "We Practice the KISS (Keep It Simple, Stupid) System."

Attempting to keep things simple is a noble endeavor; it often reflects experience with strategy and initiatives that have failed because of their complexity. When people become confused, they do nothing; and as unappealing as *that* may be, a simple, easily implemented strategy that is wrong for the marketplace may be worse. In fact, "simple," "easy," and "consistent" may mean getting it wrong every time, without exception.

Preferable, of course, would be a simple strategy that required no change or organizational learning. But as buggy whips, hula hoops, and manual typewriters prove, the needs of the marketplace change. Those who fail to respond will be left behind.

Market management does require change, because it requires greater responsiveness to the marketplace. However, there are two elements that make its implementation straightforward. One, it focuses efforts by mandating some activities and ruling out others, resulting in greater simplicity. Part of the current complexity often comes from trying to be all things to all people. Two, implementation of market management involves all front-line personnel in the local market analysis and planning. Their involvement and understanding of the market needs enhances their ability to carry it out. Rather than relying on management directives, they implement solutions and strategies that are primarily their own. They will not recommend solutions they cannot understand or act on.

These first three executive obstacles are all forms of denial. They are very debilitating to rapid, market-responsive change, and they keep the organization from learning the skills of market management.

For so many, the real issue here is fear: the fear of making a decision, of putting it all on the line. Yet what could be scarier than overseeing the loss of the franchise? In today's environment of rapid change, can there be any risk greater than that of the status quo? The organizational genocide of middle management is occurring because something other than the status quo is needed. IBM, General Motors, Westinghouse, Compaq, and American Express remove their top executives for moving too slowly — for not bringing enough market-driven change. Technology will not stand still; markets will not stand still; and neither will management. Either lead the change or get run over by it.

The next three are obstacles that appear once you decide to implement market management.

Obstacle Four: "Look, Mom, No Hands!"

Many executives fail to play the necessary role in implementation because they underestimate the significance of the organizational, cultural, and management systems changes involved. This creates two key problems. First, when the executive team is not actively involved, it implies that the strategy is transient: "This, too, shall pass." This causes some to wait out the change rather than enlist. Two, only up close does it become apparent how many of the changes require executive leadership. The new types of market goals, the different information requirements, the reward system, and many other changes must be addressed.

This does not mean that the transformation must be instantaneous. The change process must be started, but changes must be prioritized and implemented over time. For example, goals that only track product volume without attention to relationship penetration, profitability, or revenue of high-value customers will need to evolve over time. The company needs to be aware of these limitations, and know what can be addressed in the short term and what cannot. An executive or executive team that is too far from the action on these issues will sound out of touch to the troops and will miss the opportunity to perform one of the most important tasks of leadership: removing obstacles. Talking the new game of market management while tracking and rewarding the old game will not work. The executive team should actively go through one complete implementation of the market management process as a learner in order to be an informed advocate for the process.

Obstacle Five: Stuck Without a Learning Process or System

One of the most common obstacles to implementation of market management is the absence of a process to teach *why* it is critical (pain), *what* is required (remedy), and *how* to accomplish it (competence). Many businesses are stuck at a low level of competence because market management is viewed not as a new way of doing business but as a planning exercise. An effective market management process and system must deal with the why, what, and how and must provide skill, tools, and coaching to support the learning.

Obstacle Six: Poor Follow-Up

Someone once said that most companies are good at beginnings and endings but lousy at managing the middles. Just as with any strategy, it is easy to assume that a good, strong start will not require sustained follow-up. It may be preaching to the choir to say that follow-up is critical — but the truth is that it is often neglected. Effective follow-up means tracking results against market plans. It means asking the branch, store, or center manager for his plan when executives visit. It means making heroes out of those who are profitably winning their markets.

It is not as though you needed a course in how to follow up or that you won't know what to do. It is like the old adage about your sex life: "Don't be afraid it won't be perfect — just be afraid it won't be." The biggest sin is that of omission.

Obstacle Seven: Poor Integration with Other Strategies

One of the challenges of implementing any strategy is integrating it with other corporate initiatives. There are certainly any number of initiatives, but the ones you most often encounter are those dealing with service and quality, such as Total Quality Management (TQM).

Some retail executives have said that the only way to get acceptance for market management is to position it as a quality initiative. It is our belief that market management is indeed an excellent addition to a traditional quality program. When we implement our process, Managing Local Markets, we often describe it as a parallel to TQM because it brings greater market and customer responsiveness and productivity while reinforcing the tenets of quality. It also provides processes, tools, and skills for implementation. In fact, as the quality movement matures, we believe it will continue to enhance its focus on the three principles of acting local, segmenting your market, and getting breakthrough productivity.

In the final analysis, your highest priority is the *quality* that adds the greatest value to the profitable markets you wish to dominate. Market management adds a level of focus to quality that makes it more market driven, productive, and profitable. Managing Local Markets is to a market-driven culture what Total Quality Management is to a quality-driven culture. By integrating the two, you get a market-driven, quality culture.

Whether the initiative is quality, cost reduction, sales or any other, care must be taken to integrate market management as a continuation, the next step of the initiative. Otherwise, it will be interpreted as a replacement for, rather than an expansion of, the original initiative. The recommended processes and training provide a way to align and install it into the overall strategy.

OBSTACLES FOR MANAGERS

CLOSELY RELATED TO THE OBSTACLES AT THE EXECUTIVE LEVEL is a set of market management obstacles for managers. However, at each level these obstacles get somewhat redefined. As we consider regional managers, then store managers, the focus shifts more toward execution.

Before we discuss their obstacles, it is important to note that many of these managers are excited by the concept of market management. They know all too well the futility of striving for more sales, better service, less cost, and more focused targeting of markets with only the conventional tactics. The idea of getting more focused and targeted stirs in them the promise of the possible; and once they involve the whole team in the analysis and planning, they experience the benefit of a focused team that is committed to realizing the plan.

Despite these benefits, there are very real obstacles for managers, before, during, and after implementation.

Obstacle One: Not Enough Time

This is always a concern, and it is almost always a legitimate one. In fact, often *the more that time is of concern — the greater the need for market management*. However, just because the need is acute does not mean that it will be easy to find the time to analyze, plan, and implement.

Usually 60 to 100 hours of combined manager and staff time per store is required to install market management. Managers ponder where they will find the time. Yet an average store of 12 people, with about 2,000 work hours per person per year, will spend 24,000 hours doing *something*. The crucial question is, How do you make the most of those hours? What would you be willing to invest to improve the return to the customer (customer satisfaction), the employee (job satisfaction), and the shareholder (financial performance)? You cannot wave a magic wand; it must come through hard work. You must invest if you expect a return.

If the vision is clear and the payoff attractive, you can always find the time. It may be the only way to break the time trap that is such a pervasive part of business today. It is not that there isn't time, but that your time must be reallocated in order to get started. The irony in this is that, more than anything else, the outcome from market management is the permanent reallocation of time based on the market potential. There is always enough time! What is in short supply is profitable, loyal customers; productive, committed employees; better ways of operating the business; and managers who will challenge their staff and help them break out and perform at a higher level.

Obstacle Two: C Service vs. A Service

Market management requires you to define different levels of service — new options for customers — based on what customers want and are willing to pay for. Great news for customers! Right? Well, it is, but this is not always apparent. Usually the staff gets excited about providing more attentive service to the A customers. They know it's the right thing to do. They get much of their job satisfaction from serving customers who express appreciation. The rub comes in providing streamlined or less service to the C customers. It is important to acknowledge that many front-line people are in the C segment — C's "R" Us. A demeaning view of C customers can be insulting to the staff.

Since in most businesses 25 to 35 percent of the customers are currently getting more service than they are paying for, some current service expectations will probably be violated. Weaning these customers will not be easy; some of them will have become personal friends of front-line staff. If employees spend less time chatting with them, filling out their forms, dropping things off for them, or balancing their checkbooks, they may feel uncomfortable.

There is also the issue of fairness. We often hear stories like the one a teller related to her branch manager about one of her favorite customers:

> It's just not fair. Mr. Hightower is one of the wealthiest people in our community and when he bounces a check, we cover him, and then we waive the NSF [not sufficient funds] fee and everything is hunky dory. When Mrs. Hughes bounces a check, we charge her a fee. She is a widow with three kids — just barely making it. That fee is the difference between barely getting by and not. It's just not fair.

This is a sensitive issue, and it creates a real dilemma. The reality is that your best customers are already subsidizing your loss leaders. Many of them are paying for first-class service but getting coach treatment. If they take their business elsewhere, the company must either drastically increase fees and charges to the lower end or go out of business. In the long run, it is not a decision that anyone inside the company makes. The marketplace will vote over time, and that will be the way the decision is made.

It is interesting how clear we are about the different classes of customer needs in buying cars, airline seats, food products, and other items. Sometimes the truth hurts, but it is still the truth. As managers give additional information to staff — how much we make on our best customers and how much we lose on our worst customers — the truth becomes more evident.

Fairness means giving people the value they pay for. Fairness means making promises we can keep, not promises that are impossible to deliver on. Fairness means that if a customer pays us for a Cadillac, we'd better deliver a Cadillac and not a Chevy. Fairness means running the business so that if we work hard and smart, we stay in business and keep our jobs.

Yes, there is a place for charity in business, but we need to be sure we do not confuse charity with fairness. We may have customers who need our help. We can decide to help them as a select group because they need it and we feel it is the right thing to do. We can educate them as to their options. We can run a seminar for them on how to balance their checkbooks. We can define limits for them; we can refer them to social agencies; we can form a local volunteer group to help them. There are lots of options. However, we cannot give things away without a plan or goal or even a conscious decision, or dispense service preferentially to those who make the loudest demands. Even in charity, let's define and target our market based on the criteria we set, lest we be disappointed as to the recipients of our gifts. Let's select the ten customers that we shall subsidize. Random allocation of service will neither maximize profit nor maximize charity to those in need.

Making different levels of service available to our customers is good news for them and good business for the company. If we truly believe everyone should get the same level of service, then let's also insist that everyone drive the same cars, wear the same clothes, see the same doctors, and so on. Treating everyone the same will not make everyone equally satisfied.

We must be clear that *different levels* of service does not mean *bad* service; it means the best service possible for the price. Just because we buy a Chevrolet (rather than a Cadillac) doesn't mean we don't expect it to be a good car, to be functional, to start, to run. However, it will have fewer features and frills. A Chevrolet will deliver the basics about as well as a Cadillac. In fact, there is great competition for the Chevy business, and if we don't deliver value, we will lose it as a market in our local trade area. The same is true of service. We often make a distinction between quality of service and quantity of service. Accurate, reliable, efficient service is not optional — it is a minimum standard for doing business. The basic *quality* must be there, but the *quantity* of time, attention, and value-added follow-up will vary according to customers' needs and willingness to pay.

As a manager, you will face no leadership challenge that is more critical than helping your people rethink service differentiation. You will have to develop analogies, metaphors, and experiences that facilitate the new thinking.

Obstacle Three: Unlearning and Relearning the Way to Win a Market

The first step in implementing organizational change is unlearning. So much of what has driven us in the past has been one-size-fits-all approaches to customer management. As we aid our front-line staff in rethinking this paradigm, we will also have to unlearn some of our current methods and approaches and replace them with new ones.

This obstacle of unlearning and relearning would be infinitely easier if there were a common set of solutions that worked effectively across all markets. In fact, the temptation is to try to develop a single, central formula for allocating sales and service resources. However, real productivity and market dominance can be generated only by reallocating and redesigning service delivery to fit the local market.

Let's look at a retail store system. In some markets, optimal levels can be attained only by redirecting and redesigning service efforts to retain and grow seldom-seen high-value customers. In other markets, heavy solicitation of high-potential prospects is the key; in yet others, the only way is to be lean, fast, and efficient in serving C customers because they are the key to that trade area.

It is ironic that what must be learned takes us "back to the future," because this is the way small-town banks, hardware stores, and grocery stores had to operate in order to survive in their local markets — they had to take special care of their best customers. As large corporations acquired and consolidated these operations, there was a priority for installing common systems, operating procedures, and approaches — an emphasis on doing everything the same way. In the process, we lost the organizational memory for the practices that were specifically customized to local market conditions and needs.

Now we must take a step back and define what the market needs, then refine or tailor our practices, within agreed-upon limits, to meet these needs. This relearning can be done through trial and error, although the amount of time and number of errors makes this learning approach very expensive. Using a systematic process for rethinking customer management greatly improves the quality and speed of the relearning.

So, like executives, managers have a set of obstacles that can retard progress to market management: too little time, resistance to differentiated service, unlearning and relearning. They are all real, and they are not easy to overcome. This is great news if you are a middle manager! If someone could overcome them by just writing a book or sending a memo, the company would not need you. In fact, if we look at the dramatic decline in the number of middle managers throughout North America, it is, in my opinion, because they have not been able to add value to the change necessary for success in the '90s. Their traditional function of processing and passing information can now be done cheaper and faster by computers.

We have a choice: either we add value to the changes demanded by the marketplace, or the company will unbundle us and do it without us. The fact is that the change to market management needs strong management and leadership because it requires a cultural transformation. However, if managers are unable to add value to the change process, they will become less relevant and less valuable. Managers must make that choice.

In summary, the role of executives and managers is to envision change, create strategy, and implement market management. A crucial component for their success in this endeavor is the ability to remove obstacles. To the extent that these obstacles can be anticipated, we can provide the processes, tools, and skills that are designed to minimize them — designed to achieve quality by doing it right the first time.

14

The Will to Act

Leadership Born of Passion and Value

66 Hell is the state in which we are barred from receiving what we truly need because of the value we give to what we merely want. 99 [1]

— *Jacob Needleman*

*I*T IS NOT COMPLICATED. IT'S SIMPLE: the game is value. The judge is the customer. The winner is the one who brings the greatest value to the local market. The more service-oriented the business, the more it matters how the local market manager allocates and directs resources to bring the kind of value that is important to the unique needs of the local market. And in the long run, all business is service.

The shareholder's objective is profit. The company's objective is to *provide* the quality of product or service for which customers are willing to pay a profit. The customer's objective is to *receive* value that is good enough that they do not mind paying the company a profit to produce and deliver it.

Not all customers value the same things. Some want speed, others quality, convenience, price, image — it varies. And these preferences vary from trade area to trade area. Profitably winning the local market — that is, taking the best business that is available locally in terms of customers, prospects, and competitive forces — is the way to optimize the company's return. This is the job of the market manager. Doing the same thing in every market will get different results and will sub-optimize both potential profits to the business and value to local customers. Doing the right thing in each local market, within the mission and capabilities of the corporation, will maximize the return.

To win the race to deliver the best value in the local trade area, a market manager must decide which groups of customers and prospects are key to optimizing or winning the trade area; products don't make you money, customers do. To be good at the customer business, you must be truly passionate about four things:

- Retention of your best customers
- Growth of your high-potential customers
- Attraction of your target prospects
- Cost management of your price-sensitive and low-margin customers

Value does *not* mean delivering more service than customers are willing to pay for. If they are concerned about price, you are not customer driven when your *only* concern is great service; nor are you customer driven if your price is low but you give them less service than they desire. If you get the local value equation wrong, you go out of business for one of two reasons: too few customers (not enough value for them), or large losses (not enough value for the company). In either case, everyone loses.

Retention, growth, attraction, and cost management of target groups are the *vital signs* of a local store, just as they are, in aggregate, for an entire enterprise. People, premises, promotion, service promise delivery, products, and price are the critical tactics that influence these vital signs.

This is not news. We all know this. Why aren't we further along?

CHANGING THE MISSION

THE ANSWER IS that we have not made local market management our mission. We need to be *mission-driven* organizations, but all too often we are *symptom-driven*. Revenue is too low — let's focus on sales. Service is not good enough — let's focus on service quality. Costs are too high — let's focus on costs. In the short run we can always fix the symptom; but this just creates another problem. The mission is to profitably win the local market. This means we must establish connectivity for sales, service, quality, and cost strategies and make them march together under one flag.

Changing the mission means taking on the difficult task of organizational learning. "It's cultural change, stupid." Indeed it is; and it's decision time. Whether you are an executive responsible for 2,000 stores, a branch manager, a local business owner, or a salesperson with a defined trade area, it comes down to one thing — the will to act. Oswald Chambers says it plainly: "Will is the whole man active."[2] In baser terms, it is the mixture of fear and greed (with perhaps a little moral righteousness thrown in) that will overcome inertia and call us to battle.

What will give us the will to act? What are our reasons? Let me suggest three.

Reason One: For the Customer

Segmentation began not with businesses but with customers, because customers have different needs. They rule out most providers while in the process of finding the provider that best meets their needs. Local market management is simply an attempt to become the provider of choice for certain target groups in a trade area.

At its core, market management's message to the customer goes beyond, Come in and see if you like us. It says, We have designed ourselves to fit you. Yes, we are a store or a bank or an airline with some basic products, but in this local market we are viewing the world from your shoes. And we are tailoring, bending, and flexing our standard delivery (product, service) as responsively as possible to your needs. This means that, rather than one size fits all, we are looking for options we can give you — on price, service quality, and so forth — to meet your needs. And because we cannot be good at all things, we will be clear about what we cannot do.

Integrity with our customers means we are what we say we are. Promising every customer Cadillac service is something we cannot deliver on and for which many of our customers are not willing to pay. When we promise what we cannot deliver, we create a credibility problem.

What we *can* deliver to everyone is value. For those who want Cadillacs, we deliver Cadillacs, if we determine that it makes sense in our local market — and we expect to be paid accordingly, in terms of price, volume, or repeat business. For those who want Chevrolets, we provide the best value available in Chevrolets. We let the customer decide. Market management means getting clear as to the customers we wish to attract and retain in a local trade area, then becoming the best at delivering the value they want. The will to act comes out of the will to serve the customer.

Reason Two: For the Staff

We cannot serve the customer if we do not serve the employee. Market management means that we stop the sales and service waves and address the mission: to profitably win the local market. Our people are tired, stressed, and confused. They feel that in spite of their efforts the battle is being lost — and in many industries they are right. It is an impressive list, the former market leaders that are struggling: Sears, Delta, IBM, General Motors, banks, and traditional department stores are battling to survive.

Our people are working harder than ever; the loss of high-value market share is mounting; the restructuring process is painful. Everyone is trying to deliver more sales and better service at less cost, but in the many places where service has not been reengineered and reallocated for local target markets, our additional effort will not be enough. By trying to do everything, we end up doing nothing well — like many retailers, with prices too high to compete with Wal-Mart, service too plain to compete with Nordstrom, not specialized enough to compete with The Gap — working hard in the miserable, mediocre middle. It is not a winnable war.

We must redefine the war to win it. First, we must define expectations relative to the local market. In growing markets we expect more, in shrinking markets we live with less. The beauty of local market management is that there is always a way to win. We don't compare Nolan Ryan with Babe Ruth — we compare power pitchers with other power pitchers and home-run hitters with other home-run hitters. Among those in shrinking markets, who is winning? Among those in expanding markets, who is struggling?

Second, let's get proactive around winning the local market. One area manager I know got a blinding flash of the obvious when he said, "You know, we have a 1 to 7 appraisal scale here, and our branch managers can be a 5 or 6 if they can just keep the branch from blowing up." His insight was that few were managing their markets; they were just trying to keep a lid on things, managing the noise rather than the market. We need to concentrate on the mission — to profitably win the local market — and rule out the things that get in the way of proactive, focused efforts. One of the bedrock philosophies that helped Dallas Cowboys coach Jimmy Johnson energize the troops and win the 1993 Super Bowl was, "When you get ahead, attack."

An important part of focusing on the mission is ruling out things that don't fit. Part of the ruling-out process involves educating customers. One of our vendors enlightened me about this a few years back. Our company, ActionSystems, does a lot of training, and accordingly, we rely on outside printers to publish our materials. I was negotiating a large print job with a printer who had done a lot of work for us. I was trying hard to get a competitive deal and, of course, wanted a great price with high quality and fast turnaround, et cetera, et cetera. He stopped me in midsentence and said, "Robert — price, quality, speed — pick any two."

I was silenced. I was up against someone who understood the business better than I. He was clear and succinct on the tradeoff. At that moment I understood why his company was the best printer in the marketplace. He knew where to stretch — any two areas important to the customer — and where to protect his workers and his profits. It is this kind of ruling out that energizes and empowers our employees to stretch, to give their all to a game that is winnable but not waste energy on one that isn't.

Third, the company's need to perform is consistent with the employee's need to be empowered. We must put our staff back in charge and let them run their business — but not without enabling them and holding them accountable. The will to act comes out of the will to serve our staff.

Reason Three: For the Shareholder

We cannot serve customers and employees if we are not profitable. To make the business profitable, to improve return on equity, and to increase the value of the stock price are what executives and managers are paid to do. Traditionally we think of executives and board members as a group of big cigars who are the recipients of workers' toils. They benefit when things go well, of course, but they are also under great pressure to stay ahead of the market. Just ask Robert Stempel of General Motors, John Akers of IBM, Paul Legos of Westinghouse, or James Robinson of American Express — all were top executives, and all were canned in a trice. Peter Drucker quotes an old proverb: "Whom the gods want to destroy, they send 40 years of success."[3] Success can be insurmountable.

Executives must serve shareholders. I have an Aunt Minnie; perhaps you do, too. Aunt Minnie is retired and widowed, and she has her savings to feed and shelter her through the remainder of her life. Let's say she decides to invest some of those dollars in our company. Someone has told her that we know what we are doing, based on our past performance, the markets we serve, or the brilliance of our management. Whether she buys stock or invests in a mutual fund, Aunt Minnie is betting part of her future on us. As long as she is invested in us, she empowers our executive team to act in her behalf, as an absentee owner, to manage the company and its resources. Her standard of living will rise, fall, or remain stable, depending on how we do.

When we profitably win our local markets, Aunt Minnie smiles and feels comfortable buying groceries and medicine and paying the bills. However, when we lose a lot of money on certain groups of customers, lose share of wallet from our best customers, spend most of our time on the least profitable customers, fail to track which customer groups we are retaining and growing — then we begin to affect her life savings. And if it gets bad enough, Aunt Minnie will fire us. She and her fellow shareholders will sell their stock or change executive teams or both. We will have fewer resources to buy new technology, develop new products, and open new stores that would add value for our customers. As employees, we will get less compensation, less advancement potential, and less job security.

As executives and managers, we are painfully aware of the pressure to perform for Aunt Minnie. Yet very few of our front-line employees ride to work worrying about our quarterly earnings or stock price. The executive's and manager's job is to take care of employees so they will take care of customers — and to take care of the shareholders so they will take care of the employees. The will to act comes out of the will to serve the shareholders.

When we profitably win our local markets, we are profitably delivering value to our customers; we are enrolling our employees in a value-based, empowered, service-focused role that is winnable. We are bringing value to Aunt Minnie's life savings and, as a result, raising her standard of living.

GETTING STARTED

SPEED TO MARKET WITH IMPROVED LOCAL SALES AND SERVICE is no different from speed to market with a new product. Cycle time is critical. When we look across industries, virtually all of the major players are pursuing local market management strategy. Yet some have worked on it for two to three years with only limited progress. What will provide the competitive advantage they are hoping for? Will simply having a strategy for market management do it? Establishing the position of market manager? Asking for a market plan? I doubt it.

We believe the keys to getting started in market management lie in two concepts. First, we must borrow from the success of the Total Quality Management school, and "do it right the first time" by installing the right process, skills and tools up front. Many good strategies have been buried by weak implementation.

Second, in a competitive environment, speed to the marketplace is critical. Tom Peters warns, "niche or be niched." We can either preempt the competition by aggressively pursuing the most profitable segments in each local market, or we can "be niched" and take what's left. If we hesitate until we are forced to react, we must either spend money trying to reclaim profitable customers from the competition or take the lower-margin, bottom-of-the-barrel customers they didn't want.

At the risk (or the certainty) of sounding self-serving, our company believes the magnitude of the change that most businesses are seeking warrants outside help from consultants who are experienced in making it happen. We have worked with businesses that started on their own, got to a certain point, and became stuck. The talking stage was easy, but the challenge of instituting the processes, strategies, tactics, and new ways of thinking stopped them short of the cultural change. The transformation must be led by executives and managers, but just as with TQM, time-based competition, and other strategic initiatives, having access to a body of knowledge, expertise, processes, tools, practices, and skills can greatly improve the odds for success. Working with someone who has been through it before helps executives and managers anticipate obstacles and provides support and training that can be tailored to an organization's unique needs. It adds speed, quality, and certainty to the mission.

The will to act can be born of compliance or of passion. For most of us, leadership is most powerful and passionate when it comes from discovered truth. Many of us have discovered one or several truths (quality, empowerment) that can stir our passion. Too often, however, we have lacked a fuller vision that unites our discovered truths with those yet undiscovered — to paint the picture that covers the whole canvas.

Local market management takes several key mantras — quality, cost, productivity, empowerment, sales culture, customer service, reengineering, micromarketing — and ties them together. The goal? Profitably win the local market. How? Best value for the target groups. Who wins? Customers, employees, and Aunt Minnie.

Why aren't there more winners? Why do so many hit the wall? They lack the will to act. Winners do things that less successful people are unwilling to do.

Take the risk. Rule things out. Narrow the focus. Change the game. Take the initiative. Niche or be niched. Just do it. These are all phrases designed to elicit one critical response — the will to act.

CHAPTER NOTES

Introduction

1   Oswald Chambers. *My Utmost for His Highest.* Grand Rapids, Michigan: Discovery House Publishers, 1963, p. 26.

Part I

Chapter 1

1   Herbert Stein. "The Age of Ignorance." *The Wall Street Journal,* June 11, 1993, p. A10.

2   John Huey. "America's Most Successful Merchant." *Fortune,* Sept. 12, 1991, p. 46.

3   Sam Walton with John Huey. *Sam Walton: Made in America.* New York: Doubleday, 1992, p. 219.

4   Terry Maxon. "American looking at bottom line." *The Dallas Morning News,* Feb. 16, 1992, p. 1H.

5   Jim Mitchell. "Southland sprucing up 7-Eleven stores." *The Dallas Morning News,* April 18, 1993, p. 1H, 8H.

6   Gale Eisenstodt. "Information Power." *Forbes,* June 21, 1993, p. 44.

7   Lewis D. Eigen and Jonathan P. Siegel. *The Manager's Book of Quotations.* New York: AMACOM, 1989, p. 474.

8   Lynn W. Adkins. "Merrill Lynch Beckoning Bank Customers." *American Banker,* Sept. 23, 1992, p. 10.

9   Karen Benfield. "Check Cashers Are Attracting a More Affluent Clientele." *The Wall Street Journal,* Sept. 23, 1992, p B2.

10   Review & Outlook. "Bankers, Risk and the Regulators" (editorial). *The Wall Street Journal,* Dec. 16, 1992, p. A14.

11   Richard Layne. "Top Worry of CEOs: Slow Revenue Growth." *American Banker,* Sept. 4, 1992, p. 1.

12   Waino Pilh (Andersen Consulting). "The Changing Market Place." Speech at ABA Small Business Conference, 1993. Copyright © 1993, Waino Pihl.

13   Review & Outlook. "CEOs: The Vision Thing" (editorial). *The Wall Street Journal*, Jan. 28, 1993, p. A14.

Chapter 2

1   Christina Duff. "Megastores That Entertain and Educate May Signal the Future of Merchandising." *The Wall Street Journal*, March 11, 1993, p. B1.

2   Peter Drucker. "A Turnaround Primer." *The Wall Street Journal*, Feb. 2, 1993, p. A10.

Part II

Chapter 3

1   Shel Silverstein. "Smart" (poem). *Where the Sidewalk Ends*. New York: HarperCollins Publishers, 1974, p. 35.

2   Paul B. Carroll. "The Failures of Central Planning — At IBM." *The Wall Street Journal*, Jan. 28, 1993, p. A 14.

3   Dick Welsh, as told to author.

4   Frederick Reichheld and W. Earl Sasser, Jr. "Zero Defections: Quality Comes to Services." *Harvard Business Review*, Sept.–Oct. 1990, p. 108.

Chapter 4

1   Stanley Marcus. Speech delivered before the marketing department of The University of Texas at Austin, Feb. 4, 1987.

2   Jeremy Main. "Is the Baldrige Overblown?" *Fortune*, July 1, 1992, pp. 62–65.

3   Ron Winslow. "Report Card on Quality and Efficiency of HMOs May Provide a Model for Others." *The Wall Street Journal*, March 9, 1993, p. B1.

4   Philip Crosby. *Quality Without Tears*. New York: McGraw-Hill, 1984.

5   Study by Technical Assistance Research Programs (TARP), Washington, D.C., in Tom Peters. *Thriving on Chaos*. New York: Alfred A. Knopf, Inc., 1987, p. 91.

6   Karl Albrecht and Ron Zemke. *Service America! Doing Business in the New Economy*. Homewood, Illinois: Dow Jones-Irwin, 1985, pp. 19–47.

7   Jan Carlzon. *Moments of Truth*. Cambridge, Mass.: Ballinger Publishing Co., 1987, pp. 21–30.

8   Thomas J. Peters and Robert H. Waterman, Jr. *In Search of Excellence*. New York: Harper & Row, 1982.

9   John Huey. "Nothing Is Impossible." *Fortune*, Sept. 23, 1991, p. 138.

10 Peters and Waterman. Also *In Search of Excellence — The Film*, a John Nathan and Sam Tyler Production based on the book by Peters and Waterman.

11 Bruce Little. "Guru has a passion for slashing managers." Toronto *Globe and Mail*.

12 William H. Davidow and Bro Uttal. "Service Companies: Focus or Falter." *Harvard Business Review*, July–Aug. 1989, p. 77.

13 Thomas H. Davenport. *Process Innovation: Reengineering Work through Information Technology*. Boston: Harvard Business School Press, 1993, p. 117.

Chapter 5

1   "Candle in the Wind" (song). Written by Elton John and Bernie Taupin. Copyright © 1973, Songs of PolyGram International, Inc. Used by permission. All rights reserved.

2   Lee Berton. "Ernst Pact May Have Given FDIC Leverage to Challenge Other Firms." *The Wall Street Journal*, Dec. 3, 1992, p. B11.

3   Study by Technical Assistance Research Programs (TARP), Washington, D.C.

4   Council on Financial Competition. *Zero Defections: Perfecting Customer Retention & Recovery*. Washington, D.C.: The Advisory Board Company, 1990, pp. 3–18. (Related article: Frederick Reichheld and W. Earl Sasser, Jr. "Zero Defections: Quality Comes to Services." *Harvard Business Review*, Sept.–Oct. 1990, pp. 105–111.)

5   Ibid.

6   Bain & Company Strategic Consulting, Boston, Mass. Council on Financial Competition. *Zero Defections: Perfecting Customer Retention & Recovery*. Washington, D.C.: The Advisory Board Company, 1990, p. 45.

7   Ibid.

8   Sanford Rose. "Retail Bankers Must Review Their ABCs" (Comment). *American Banker*, June 27, 1991, p. 1.

9   David Birch. "The Hidden Economy." *The Wall Street Journal Reports*, June 10, 1988, p. 23R.

Chapter 6

1   David A. Aaker. *Developing Business Strategies* (2nd Edition). New York: John Wiley & Sons, 1988, p. 21.

2   Jonathan Dahl. "Travel Agents' Fare Share Soars as Airlines Log Losses." *The Wall Street Journal*, Tuesday, Feb. 23, 1993, p. B1.

3   Al Ehrbar. "'Reengineering' Gives Firms New Efficiency, Workers the Pink Slip." *The Wall Street Journal*, March 16, 1993. p. A11.

4   Robert D. Buzzel and Bradley T. Gale. *The PIMS Principles: Linking Strategy to Performance*. New York: The Free Press, 1987.

Part III

1   Robert J. Samuelson. "A Shakeout in Services: Cutbacks will continue as the economy recovers." *Newsweek*, Aug. 5, 1991, p. 65.

2   Del Jones. "Southwest soars on busiest routes." *USA Today*, May 12, 1993, p. 2B.

Chapter 7

1   Theodore Levitt. *The Marketing Imagination* (new, expanded edition). New York: The Free Press, 1986.

2   Sam Walton with John Huey. *Sam Walton: Made in America*. New York: Doubleday, 1992, pp. 219–221.

3   Ibid., p. 220.

4   Ram Charan. "How Networks Reshape Organizations — For Results." *Harvard Business Review*, Sept.–Oct. 1991, p. 110.

5   Guy Webster (*Arizona Republic*). "Xerox hands power to the little guy." *The Dallas Morning News*, Sunday, Oct. 18, 1992, p. 3H.

6   Pat Baldwin. "Grocer's performance tamer than expected one year after entering D-FW market." *The Dallas Morning News*, Feb. 15, 1992, p. 1D.

7   Ibid., p. 4D.

8   Merril Stevenson. "Wooing the Customer." (International Banking Survey.) *The Economist*, March 28, 1986, p. 9.

9   Kent Pelz. "It Pays to Think Small in Marketing." *American Banker*, March 4, 1992, p. 4.

10   Richard Gibson. "Broad Grocery Price Cuts May Not Pay." *The Wall Street Journal*, May 7, 1993, p. B1.

11   Laurence Hooper. "CD Ventures Are Set by IBM, Blockbuster." *The Wall Street Journal*, May 11, 1993, pp. B1, B6.

12   Gregory A. Patterson. "Sears Roebuck Plans $4 Billion in Renovations." *The Wall Street Journal*, Friday, Feb. 12, 1993, p. A3.

13   Peter F. Drucker. *Management: Tasks, Responsibilities, Practices*. New York: Harper & Row, 1974, p. 270.

14   Charles Handy. "Balancing Corporate Power: A New Federalist Paper." *Harvard Business Review*, Nov.–Dec. 1992, p. 60.

Chapter 8

1   John O. Stevens (ed.). *In* Richard Bandler and John Grinder. *Frogs into Princes: Neuro Linguistic Programming*. Moab, Utah: Real People Press, 1979, pp. iii–iv.

2   Greg Steinmetz. "Met Life, in Switch of Strategy, Plans to Press for Sales to Affluent Customers." *The Wall Street Journal*, June 4, 1993, p. A4.

3   Pat Baldwin. "Soft-drink companies go hard sell." *The Dallas Morning News*, April 4, 1992, pp. 1F, 3F.

4   David Ansen and Charles Fleming. "Hollywood: We Stink." *Newsweek*, March 1, 1993, p. 80.

5   Kathleen Deveny. "Cold Remedies Take a Turn for the Worse." *The Wall Street Journal*, Nov. 17, 1992, p. B1.

6   Scott Feschuk. "Cola superpower battles insurgents." *The Globe and Mail*, March 9, 1993, p. B4.

7   Faye Rice. "What Intelligent Consumers Want." *Fortune*, Dec. 28, 1992, p. 57.

8   Ibid.

9   Michael Treacy and Fred Wiersema. "Customer Intimacy and Other Value Disciplines." *Harvard Business Review*, Jan.–Feb. 1993, p. 89.

10   Matthew Wald. "Leaving Some Customers at the Counter." *The New York Times*, July 19, 1992, p. 10F.

11   Ibid.

12   Kevin Goldman. "Agencies Fire Clients That Don't Pay Off." *The Wall Street Journal*, Nov. 17, 1992, p. B1.

13   Ken Graham (ed.). Financial Marketing Research Report. *Journal of Retail Banking*, Summer 1992, p. 17.

14   Council on Financial Competition. "Critical Market Share." *World Class Retail Bank Performance: Five Practices of Top-Performing Retail Banks* (Report). Washington, D.C.: The Advisory Board Company, 1992, p. 29.

15   Matthew S. Olson and Kevin T. Murray. "Does Your Retail Business Measure Up?" *American Banker*, Oct. 7, 1992, p. 4.

16   Teri Agins. "Department Stores Try to Boost Service — but Cheaply." *The Wall Street Journal*, Dec. 16, 1992, p. B3.

17   Ibid.

18   Kimberly Blanton. "Vanguard challenges powerhouse Fidelity on its own turf." *Boston Globe*, Nov. 29, 1992.

19   O. A. ("Bum") Phillips, as heard on television.

20   Stanley Marcus. Speech delivered before the marketing department of The University of Texas at Austin, Feb. 4, 1987.

21   Alan Deutschman. "Bill Gates' Next Challenge." *Fortune*, Dec. 28, 1992, p. 32.

22   Ibid., pp. 32, 34.

23   Ibid., p. 36.

Chapter 9

1   Al Ehrbar. "'Reengineering' Gives Firms New Efficiency Workers the Pink Slip." *The Wall Street Journal*, Tuesday, March 16, 1993, p. A11.

2   Ibid.

3   Council on Financial Competition. *Zero Defections: Perfecting Customer Retention & Recovery*. Washington, D.C.: The Advisory Board Company, 1990, p. 39.

4   Ibid., p. 14.

5   Ibid.

6   Peter Drucker. "Permanent Cost Cutting." *The Wall Street Journal*, Jan. 11, 1991, p. A10.

7   Peter Drucker. "A Turnaround Primer." *The Wall Street Journal*, Feb. 2, 1993, p. A10.

Part IV

Chapter 10

1   David Kearns, former CEO of Xerox Corp.

2   Michael Porter. *Competitive Advantage: Creating and Sustaining Superior Performance*. New York: Free Press, 1985; *and*
      Michael Porter. *Competitive Strategy: Techniques for Analyzing Industries and Competitors*. New York: Free Press, 1980.

3   Peter M. Senge. *The Fifth Discipline: The Art and Practice of the Learning Organization*. New York: Doubleday, 1990.

4   Sam Walton with John Huey. *Sam Walton: Made in America*. New York: Doubleday, 1992.

5   George Bernard Shaw. *Maxims for Revolutionists*.

6   Ronald Henkoff. "Companies That Train Best." *Fortune*, March 22, 1993, p. 63.

7 Daryl R. Conner. *Managing at the Speed of Change*. New York: Villard Books, 1993, p. 98.

8 Thomas H. Davenport. *Process Innovation: Reengineering Work through Information Technology*. Boston: Harvard Business School Press, 1993, p. 10.

9 Peter F. Drucker. "Be Data Literate — Know What to Know." *The Wall Street Journal*, Dec. 1, 1992, p. A16.

Chapter 11

1 Keith Miller. *Habitations of Dragons: Meditations for Men*. Tarrytown, New York: Fleming H. Revell Company, 1992, p. 171.

2 Michael Treacy and Fred Wiersema. "Customer Intimacy and Other Value Disciplines." *Harvard Business Review*, Jan.–Feb. 1993, p. 86.

3 As told to author by Dr. Paul S. Nadler.

4 Associated Press. "Corporations evolve to compete in '90s." *The Dallas Morning News*, Jan. 2, 1993, p. 2F.

Chapter 12

1 John Marks Templeton and James Ellison (Eds.). *Riches for the Mind and Spirit: John Marks Templeton's Treasury of Words to Help, Inspire, and Live By*. New York: Harper Collins Publishers in assoc. with The K. S. Giniger Co., 1990, p. 96.

2 Michael Treacy and Fred Wiersema. "Customer Intimacy and Other Value Disciplines." *Harvard Business Review*, Jan.–Feb. 1993, p. 89.

3 Herbert Stein. "The Age of Ignorance." *The Wall Street Journal*, June 11, 1993, p. A10.

Chapter 13

1 John Marks Templeton and James Ellison (Eds.). *Riches for the Mind and Spirit: John Marks Templeton's Treasury of Words to Help, Inspire, and Live By*. New York: Harper Collins Publishers in assoc. with The K. S. Giniger Co., 1990, pp. 44–45.

2 Stephen R. Covey. *The Seven Habits of Highly Effective People*. New York: Simon and Schuster, 1989.

3 Thomas M. Inge. *Comics as Culture*. Jackson, Miss.: University Press of Mississippi, 1990, p. 26 (Walt Kelly, *Pogo*, 1971).

Chapter 14

1 Jacob Needleman. *Money and the Meaning of Life*. New York: Doubleday, 1992.

2 Oswald Chambers. *My Utmost for His Highest*. Grand Rapids, Michigan: Discovery House Publishers, 1963, p. 138.

3 Peter Drucker. "A Turnaround Primer." *The Wall Street Journal*, Feb. 2, 1993, p. A10.

BIBLIOGRAPHY

Aaker, David A. *Developing Business Strategies* (2nd Edition). New York: John Wiley & Sons, 1988.

Adkins, Lynn W. "Merrill Lynch Beckoning Bank Customers." *American Banker*, Sept. 23, 1992, p. 10.

Agins, Teri. "Department Stores Try to Boost Service — but Cheaply." *The Wall Street Journal*, Dec. 16, 1992, pp. B1, B3.

Albrecht, Karl, and Ron Zemke. *Service America! Doing Business in the New Economy*. Homewood, Illinois: Dow Jones–Irwin, 1985.

Ansen, David, and Charles Fleming. "Hollywood: We Stink." *Newsweek*, March 1, 1993, p. 80.

Baldwin, Pat. "Grocer's performance tamer than expected one year after entering D–FW market." *The Dallas Morning News*, Feb. 15, 1992, p. D1.

Baldwin, Pat. "Soft-drink companies go hard sell." *The Dallas Morning News*, April 4, 1992, pp. 1F, 3F.

Bandler, Richard, and John Grinder; John O. Stevens (ed.). *Frogs into Princes: Neuro Linguistic Programming*. Moab, Utah: Real People Press, 1979.

Benfield, Karen. "Check Cashers Are Attracting a More Affluent Clientele." *The Wall Street Journal*, Sept. 23, 1992, p. B2.

Berton, Lee. "Ernst Pact May Have Given FDIC Leverage to Challenge Other Firms." *The Wall Street Journal*, Nov. 3, 1992, p. B11.

Birch, David. "The Hidden Economy." *The Wall Street Journal Reports*, June 10, 1988, p. 23R.

Blanton, Kimberly. "Vanguard challenges powerhouse Fidelity on its own turf." *The Dallas Morning News*, Dec. 20, 1992, p. 3H.

Buzzel, Robert D., and Bradley T. Gale. *The PIMS Principles: Linking Strategy to Performance*. New York: The Free Press, 1987.

Bryan, Lowell W. *Breaking Up the Bank: Rethinking an Industry Under Siege*. Homewood, Illinois: Dow Jones–Irwin, 1988.

Carlzon, Jan. *Moments of Truth*. Cambridge, Massachusetts: Ballinger Publishing Company, 1987.

Carroll, Paul B. "The Failures of Central Planning — At IBM." *The Wall Street Journal*, Jan. 28, 1993, p. A14.

Chambers, Oswald. *My Utmost for His Highest*. Grand Rapids, Michigan: Discovery House Publishers, 1963.

Charan, Ram. "How Networks Reshape Organizations — For Results." *Harvard Business Review*, Sept.–Oct. 1991, p. 110.

Conner, Daryl R. *Managing at the Speed of Change*. New York: Villard Books, 1993.

Council on Financial Competition. *World Class Retail Bank Performance: Five Practices of Top-Performing Retail Banks*. Washington, D.C.: The Advisory Board Company, 1992.

Council on Financial Competition. *Zero Defections: Perfecting Customer Retention & Recovery*. Washington, D.C.: The Advisory Board Company, 1990.

Covey, Stephen R. *The Seven Habits of Highly Effective People*. New York: Simon and Schuster, 1989.

Crosby, Philip. *Quality is Free*. New York: McGraw-Hill, 1979.

Crosby, Philip. *Quality Without Tears*. New York: McGraw-Hill, 1984.

Dahl, Jonathan. "Travel Agents' Fare Share Soars as Airlines Log Losses." *The Wall Street Journal*, Feb. 23, 1993, p. B1.

Davenport, Thomas H. *Process Innovation: Reengineering Work through Information Technology*. Boston: Harvard Business School Press, 1993.

Davidow, William H., and Bro Uttal. "Service Companies: Focus or Falter." *Harvard Business Review*, Jul.–Aug. 1989, p. 77 ff.

Deutschman, Alan. "Bill Gates' Next Challenge." *Fortune*, Dec. 28, 1992, p. 32.

Deveny, Kathleen. "Cold Remedies Take a Turn for the Worse." *The Wall Street Journal*, Nov. 17, 1992, p. B1.

Drucker, Peter F. "A Turnaround Primer." *The Wall Street Journal*, Feb. 2, 1993, p. A10.

Drucker, Peter F. "Be Data Literate — Know What to Know." *The Wall Street Journal*, Dec. 1, 1992, p. A16.

Drucker, Peter F. *Management: Tasks, Responsibilities, Practices*. New York: Harper & Row, 1974.

Drucker, Peter F. "Permanent Cost Cutting." *The Wall Street Journal*, Jan. 11, 1991, p. A10.

Duff, Christina. "Megastores That Entertain and Educate May Signal the Future of Merchandising." *The Wall Street Journal*, March 11, 1993, p. B1.

Ehrbar, Al. "'Reengineering' Gives Firms New Efficiency, Workers the Pink Slip." *The Wall Street Journal*, March 16, 1993, pp. A1, A11.

Eigen, Lewis D., and Jonathan P. Siegel. *The Manager's Book of Quotations*. New York: AMACOM, 1989.

Eisenstodt, Gale. "Information Power." *Forbes*, June 21, 1993, pp. 44–45.

Feschuk, Scott. "Cola superpower battles insurgents." *The Globe and Mail*, March 9, 1993, p. B4.

Gibson, Richard. "Broad Grocery Price Cuts May Not Pay." *The Wall Street Journal*, May 7, 1993, p. B1.

Goldman, Kevin. "Agencies Fire Clients That Don't Pay Off." *The Wall Street Journal*, Nov. 17, 1992, p. B1.

Graham, Ken (ed.). Financial Marketing Research Report. *Journal of Retail Banking*, Summer 1992, p. 17.

Handy, Charles. "Balancing Corporate Power: A New Federalist Paper." *Harvard Business Review*, Nov.–Dec. 1992, p. 60.

Henkoff, Ronald. "Companies That Train Best." *Fortune*, March 22, 1993, p.63.

Hooper, Laurence. "CD Ventures Are Set by IBM, Blockbuster." *The Wall Street Journal*, May 11, 1993, pp. B1, B6.

Huey, John. "America's Most Successful Merchant." *Fortune*, Sept. 12, 1991, p. 46.

Huey, John. "Nothing Is Impossible." *Fortune*, Sept. 23, 1991, pp. 135–140.

Inge, Thomas M. *Comics as Culture*. Jackson, Miss.: University Press of Mississippi, 1990.

Jones, Del. "Southwest soars on busiest routes." *USA Today*, May 12, 1993, p. 2B.

Layne, Richard. "Top Worry of CEOs: Slow Revenue Growth." *American Banker*, Sept. 4, 1992, p. 1.

Levitt, Theodore. *The Marketing Imagination* (new, expanded edition) New York: The Free Press, 1986.

Main, Jeremy. "Is the Baldrige Overblown?" *Fortune*, July 1, 1992, pp. 62–65.

Maxon, Terry. "American looking at bottom line." *The Dallas Morning News*, Feb. 16, 1992, p. 1H.

Miller, Keith. *Habitations of Dragons: Meditations for Men*. Tarrytown, New York: Fleming H. Revell Company, 1992.

Mitchell, Jim. "Southland sprucing up 7-Eleven stores." *The Dallas Morning News*, April 18, 1993, p. 1H.

Needleman, Jacob. *Money and the Meaning of Life*. New York: Doubleday, 1992.

Olson, Matthew S., and Kevin T. Murray. "Does Your Retail Business Measure Up?" *American Banker*, Oct. 7, 1992, p. 4.

Patterson, Gregory A. "Sears Roebuck Plans $4 Billion In Renovations." *The Wall Street Journal*, Feb. 12, 1993, p. A3.

Pelz, Kent. "It Pays to Think Small in Marketing." *American Banker*, March 4, 1992, p. 4.

Peters, Thomas J. *In Search of Excellence — The Film*. Produced by John Nathan and Sam Tyler.

Peters, Thomas J. *Thriving on Chaos*. New York: Alfred A. Knopf, Inc., 1987.

Peters, Thomas J., and Robert H. Waterman, Jr. *In Search of Excellence*. New York: Harper & Row, 1982.

Porter, Michael. *Competitive Advantage: Creating and Sustaining Superior Performance*. New York: Free Press, 1985.

Porter, Michael. *Competitive Strategy: Techniques for Analyzing Industries and Competitors*. New York: Free Press, 1980.

Reichheld, Frederick, and W. Earl Sasser, Jr. "Zero Defections: Quality Comes to Services." *Harvard Business Review,* Sept.–Oct. 1990, p. 108.

Review & Outlook. "Bankers, Risk and the Regulators" (editorial). *The Wall Street Journal,* Dec. 16, 1992, p. A14.

Review & Outlook. "CEOs: The Vision Thing" (editorial). *The Wall Street Journal,* Jan. 28, 1993, p. A14.

Rice, Faye. "What Intelligent Consumers Want." *Fortune,* Dec. 28, 1992, p. 57.

Rose, Sanford. "Retail Bankers Must Review Their ABCs" (comment). *American Banker,* June 27, 1991, p. 1.

Samuelson, Robert J. "A Shakeout in Services: Cutbacks will continue as the economy recovers." *Newsweek,* Aug. 5, 1991, pp. 64–65.

Senge, Peter M. *The Fifth Discipline: The Art and Practice of the Learning Organization.* New York: Doubleday, 1990.

Silverstein, Shel. *Where the Sidewalk Ends.* New York: HarperCollins Publishers, 1974.

Stein, Herbert. "The Age of Ignorance." *The Wall Street Journal,* June 11, 1993, p. A10.

Steinmetz, Greg. "Met Life, in Switch of Strategy, Plans To Press for Sales to Affluent Customers." *The Wall Street Journal,* June 4, 1993, p. A4.

Stevenson, Merril. "Wooing the Customer" (International Banking Survey). *The Economist,* March 28, 1986, p. 9.

Technical Assistance Research Programs (TARP), Washington, D.C.

Templeton, John Marks, and James Ellison (Eds.). *Riches for the Mind and Spirit: John Marks Templeton's Treasury of Words to Help, Inspire, and Live By.* New York: HarperCollins Publishers in assoc. with The K. S. Giniger Co., 1990.

Treacy, Michael, and Fred Wiersema. "Customer Intimacy and Other Value Disciplines." *Harvard Business Review,* Jan.–Feb. 1993, pp. 84–93.

Wald, Matthew. "Leaving Some Customers at the Counter." *The New York Times,* July 19, 1992, p. 10F.

Walton, Sam, with John Huey. *Sam Walton: Made in America.* New York: Doubleday, 1992.

Webster, Guy (*Arizona Republic*). "Xerox hands power to the little guy." *The Dallas Morning News,* Oct. 18, 1992, p. 3H.

Winslow, Ron. "Report Card on Quality and Efficiency of HMOs May Provide a Model for Others." *The Wall Street Journal,* March 9, 1993, p. B1.

INDEX

ABOUT THE AUTHOR

R OBERT E. HALL, a well-known consultant to industry, cofounded ActionSystems Inc. in 1979. Currently, he is CEO of the privately held, Dallas-based company. During the past decade, ActionSystems has become one of the country's leading training and consulting firms. The ActionSystems client base includes more than 30 of the Forbes top 100 companies and 11 of the top 15 banks in North America.

The effectiveness of its training programs and initiatives in helping clients translate strategy into action has been recognized by *Training Magazine* and the Instructional Systems Association. ActionSystems' models for local market management also were published in 1992 by the Council on Financial Competition in a study titled *Upgrading the Quality of Branch Management: New Approaches for Training Branch CEOs.*

Robert E. Hall has made presentations to numerous national and international conferences and organizations, including the American Society for Training and Development, the American Bankers Association, and the Retail Council of Canada. Mr. Hall's views have been published periodically in *American Banker.* He is a member of the University of Texas at Dallas School of Management Advisory Board.

Mr. Hall was formerly manager of human resource consulting for the Dallas office of Arthur Young and Company and a management development specialist at GTE; he taught two years at Oklahoma State University while completing his master's degree in organization communication. He is married and has two children.

The author may be contacted at the following address and phone:

Robert E. Hall, CEO
ActionSystems Inc.
13155 Noel Road, Suite 1700
Dallas, Texas 75240
(972) 385-0680   fax (972) 239-3534